Disastrous Decisions

The Human and Organisational Causes of the Gulf of Mexico Blowout

Andrew Hopkins

DISCLAIMER

No person should rely on the contents of this publication without first obtaining advice from a qualified professional person. This publication is sold on the terms and understanding that (1) the authors, consultants and editors are not responsible for the results of any actions taken on the basis of information in this publication, nor for any error in or omission from this publication; and (2) the publisher is not engaged in rendering legal, accounting, professional or other advice or services. The publisher, and the authors, consultants and editors, expressly disclaim all and any liability and responsibility to any person, whether a purchaser or reader of this publication or not, in respect of anything, and of the consequences of anything, done or omitted to be done by any such person in reliance, whether wholly or partially, upon the whole or any part of the contents of this publication. Without limiting the generality of the above, no author, consultant or editor shall have any responsibility for any act or omission of any other author, consultant or editor.

Disastrous Decisions

The Human and Organisational Causes
of the Gulf of Mexico Blowout

Andrew Hopkins

CCH AUSTRALIA LIMITED

GPO Box 4072, Sydney, NSW 2001

Head Office North Ryde
Phone: (02) 9857 1300 Fax: (02) 9857 1600

Customer Support
Phone: 1 300 300 224 Fax: 1 300 306 224
www.cch.com.au

Book Code: 39368A

CCH
a Wolters Kluwer business

ABOUT CCH AUSTRALIA LIMITED

CCH Australia is a leading provider of accurate, authoritative and timely information services for professionals. Our position as the "professional's first choice" is built on the delivery of expert information that is relevant, comprehensive and easy to use.

We are a member of the Wolters Kluwer group, a leading global information services provider with a presence in more than 25 countries in Europe, North America and Asia Pacific.

CCH — *The Professional's First Choice.*

Enquiries are welcome on 1300 300 224, or (for customers calling from outside Australia) +61 2 9857 1300.

Books may be purchased through CCH Australia Limited's online bookstore at www.cch.com.au.

National Library of Australia Cataloguing-in-Publication entry

Hopkins, Andrew, 1945-

Disastrous decisions: the human and organisational causes of the Gulf of Mexico blowout/by Andrew Hopkins.

ISBN: 978 1 921948 77 0 (pbk).

Subjects: BP (Firm)

        Decision making

        Petroleum industry and trade — Management

        Oil spills — Mexico, Gulf of — Management

        Industrial accidents — Mexico, Gulf of

        Environmental disasters — Mexico, Gulf of

        Emergency management — Mexico, Gulf of

        Petroleum industry and trade — Accidents — Mexico, Gulf of

        BP Deepwater Horizon Explosion and Oil Spill, 2010

Dewey Number: 363.11962233819

© 2012 CCH Australia Limited

Published by CCH Australia Limited

First published May 2012

Printed in Australia by McPherson's Printing Group

CONTENTS

CCH ACKNOWLEDGMENTS

CCH Australia Limited wishes to thank the following who contributed to and supported this publication:

Managing Director
Matthew Sullivan

Director, Books
Jonathan Seifman

Publisher, Books
Andrew Campbell

Editor
Deborah Powell

Project Coordinator
Fiona Harmsworth

Books Coordinator
Caitlin Caldwell

**Market Development Manager —
Books, Education & Mobile Content**
Lauren Ma

Indexer
Graham Clayton, Word Class Indexing & Editing

Cover Designer
Mathias Johansson

(Note: Front cover photograph — CCH has been unable to identify the copyright holder; back cover photograph — reproduced by permission of copyright holder.)

Typesetting
Midland Typesetters

ABOUT THE AUTHOR

Andrew Hopkins is Emeritus Professor of Sociology at the Australian National University (ANU) in Canberra. Over the past 20 years, he has been involved in various major accident inquiries and has undertaken consultancy work for government agencies and large companies. Andrew speaks regularly to audiences around the world about the causes of major accidents.

In 2008, Andrew received the European Process Safety Centre prize for his extraordinary contribution to process safety in Europe. This was the first time the prize was awarded to someone outside Europe.

Andrew has written a number of books, including: *Making Safety Work: Getting Management Commitment to Occupational Health and Safety* and *Managing Major Hazards: The Moura Mine Disaster* — both of which were published by Allen & Unwin.

He has also written the following books which were published by CCH Australia Limited:

- *Lessons from Longford: the Esso Gas Plant Explosion*
- *Lessons from Longford: the Trial*
- *Safety, Culture and Risk*
- *Lessons from Gretley: Mindful Leadership and the Law*
- *Failure to Learn: the BP Texas City Refinery Disaster,* and
- *Learning from High Reliability Organisations.*

Andrew has a BSc and an MA from ANU, and a PhD from the University of Connecticut. He is also a Fellow of the Safety Institute of Australia.

Andrew may be contacted on the following email address:

Andrew.Hopkins@anu.edu.au

AUTHOR ACKNOWLEDGMENTS

I would like to acknowledge the very useful conversations and email exchanges I had with many people, among others: Bob Bea, Earl Carnes, Jan Hayes, Kevin Lacy, David Llewelyn, Wayne Needoba, David Pritchard, John Smith, John Thorogood, and Jan Erik Vinnem. The working papers from the Deepwater Horizon Study Group, based in Berkeley, proved invaluable.

Thanks to the following readers whose comments helped improve this book: Jan Hayes, Anthony Hopkins, Tamar Hopkins, Heather McGregor, Sally Traill and Stephen Young.

Thanks, also, to Deborah Powell whose editing was both meticulous and sensitive to my concerns.

My deepest gratitude goes to my partner in life, Heather, without whom I could not have written this book.

CHAPTER 1

INTRODUCTION

The blowout in the Gulf of Mexico on the evening of 20 April 2010 caught everyone by surprise, although it shouldn't have.

The *Deepwater Horizon*, a huge floating drilling rig, had just completed drilling an ultra-deep well. It was operating in water that was 1.5 km (5,000 ft) deep and it had drilled to 4 km (13,000 ft) below the sea floor. This is a total depth of 5.5 km (18,000 ft) below sea level, greater than the height of the highest mountains in the United Sates, except Mt McKinley in Alaska, which rises a little over 6 km (20,300 ft) above sea level. This was an impressive achievement, although it was by no means the deepest well that the *Deepwater Horizon* had drilled.

Drilling was a long way behind schedule, but the job was finally finished and, with a sense of relief, people were preparing for departure. Suddenly, at 9.45 pm, drilling fluid — "mud" in industry language — began spewing out of the top of the derrick, covering the deck of the rig and even landing on a supply vessel stationed nearby. But worse than that, the mud was accompanied by oil and gas. Gas alarms sounded, and the vessel's engines began revving as gas reached the engine room. Almost immediately, there was an explosion, followed shortly by another. The rig was now an inferno, with flames roaring up into the night sky. There was chaos and panic. Dazed and injured people converged on the lifeboats. At least one seriously injured man was pulled from underneath rubble, loaded onto a stretcher and carried to the lifeboats. The boats were progressively lowered into the water, but some people were so afraid that they jumped 40 m (125 ft) to the sea below. The supply vessel had backed off a short distance when the mud began raining down; it launched its own rescue craft to pick up survivors in the water and took on board all of the people in lifeboats. Of the 126 people who had been on board the *Deepwater Horizon*, 115 were rescued. Eleven perished in the explosions and fire. Firefighting vessels rushed to the scene and poured water onto the *Deepwater Horizon* but the fire was uncontrollable and, two days later, the rig sank.

This was not only a disaster in terms of loss of life, it was also an environmental disaster. After the blowout erupted, but before the vessel was abandoned, efforts were made to stem the flow by activating the blowout preventer (BOP), located on the sea floor. But the BOP failed to function as intended and the flow continued unabated. It was 87 days before the well was finally capped and the flow stopped. The well was 77 km (48 miles) off the coast of Louisiana, but containment efforts were unable to prevent the oil from reaching the shores of several states around the Gulf of Mexico, doing untold damage to the environment and to the livelihood of Gulf residents.

Shares in the operating company, BP, lost half their value and, at one point, it seemed possible that the company might not survive. Two years later, the share price was still nearly 25% below its pre-blowout level. BP has estimated that it will have to pay out more than $40b in damage claims and penalties.[1]

I will say no more here about the disastrous consequences of the blowout; it is the events leading up to the blowout that will be of interest in this book.

The day of the disaster had begun well, or so it seemed. Very early that morning, the crew had finished cementing the bottom of the well. The prime purpose of this cement job was to prevent a blowout. Pumping cement 5.5 km to the bottom of a well and positioning it correctly requires considerable finesse, and engineers had spent days planning just how they would do this. Unfortunately, the cement job failed but, tragically, they did not realise it had failed, and at 5.45 am, just 16 hours before the well erupted, the cement job was declared a success.

This meant, among other things, that the team was able to dispense with a particular cement evaluation test, and contractors who had been on standby to perform the test were sent ashore on an 11 am helicopter flight.

At 8 pm, another test — a well integrity test — was completed, and the crew mistakenly declared that the well had passed the test.

Finally, in the hour before the well erupted, there were indications of what was about to occur, but these indications were missed because no one was monitoring the well. So it was that the blowout came as a complete surprise.

There have been more than a dozen books written about this disaster. Many of them focus on environmental issues. They view the blowout as a catastrophic oil spill, and there is a suggestion in many of them that the ultimate cause of this event is our reliance on oil. They conclude that the best way to prevent similar disasters in the future is to reduce that reliance. Be that as it may, there is much to be learnt from this incident about how catastrophic risks can be managed more effectively, without abandoning the hazardous activity altogether.

A related theme in some books is that the accident was the result of operating at the limits of known technology, or even beyond. On this view, drilling in deep water is just as technically challenging, and hence just as risky, as space travel. The fact is, however, that both of the space shuttle accidents, *Challenger* and *Columbia*, are better viewed as the result of organisational failure rather than technological complexity.[2] We shall see that the same is true for the Gulf of Mexico blowout.

A final theme is that the well owner, BP, was somehow a bad company, a rogue, an industry outlier. This kind of analysis echoes public sentiment: the incident generated massive public outrage for which BP was a lightning rod. But viewing BP as an industry outlier just doesn't fit the facts. Two other major companies were involved — Transocean, the owner of the drilling rig, and Halliburton, the service company responsible for cementing the well. Both of these companies were implicated, in the sense that, had they behaved differently, the accident would not have happened. This was very much a drilling industry accident. Some of these popular accounts are discussed in more detail in Chapter 11.

All this raises the ticklish issue of how the incident should be named. Was it the *BP* oil spill, as several book titles suggest? To describe it in this way seems unavoidably to play into the hands of those who seek to stir up moral outrage against BP. Should the accident be named after the rig, the *Deepwater Horizon*? That is how BP titled its report, which suggests an alternative view about where responsibility lies. Several books refer to *Deepwater Horizon* in their titles, perhaps because it facilitated word plays such as "fire on the horizon" and "disaster on the horizon". More neutral is the name of the well itself — Macondo. Not one of the books uses "Macondo" in its title, presumably because the name is not well known. But various inquiry report titles do use this name, thereby avoiding any suggestion of taking sides. In this book, I shall refer to the Macondo incident, the Macondo team and so on, partly because of the neutrality of the name, but also because it is a convenient and accurate way of referring to the drilling team, which included personnel from various companies.

Apart from the outpouring of popular writing, an unprecedented number of reports have been written about the disaster, some by government and quasi-governmental agencies and some by the companies involved. These provide a wealth of invaluable detail about the technical causes of the incident. But that very detail makes them hard for industry outsiders to read. Ploughing through them amounts to taking a crash course in drilling engineering. My book is addressed to audiences both inside and outside the industry and seeks to minimise technical detail in order to maximise comprehensibility. I do not shy away from technical detail, however, when that is necessary to make sense of the decisions that were made.

The other feature of most of the reports is that, while they provide detailed accounts of *what* happened, they do not focus on *why* it happened. Answering the *why* question takes us into the realm of human and organisational factors, which was not the centre of attention in most of the inquiries. It is certainly important to know what people *did*, but even more important to know *why* they did it.

It is not enough to know that people made mistakes; we need to know why they made these mistakes if we are to have any hope of preventing them or others from making the same mistakes again. The decision-makers invariably thought they were doing the right thing, when in fact their flawed decisions were taking them a step at a time towards disaster. We need to make sense of those disastrous decisions, which means understanding why they made sense to the decision-maker. Very often, the way people make sense of a situation dictates how they act, which means that they are not really engaged in decision-making at all.[3] So this book is an attempt to get inside the heads of decision-makers and understand how they themselves understood the situations they were in. Furthermore, it seeks to discover what it was in their organisational environment that encouraged them to think and act as they did.

Thinking about accident causation

Initial attempts to explain the accident focused on the failure of a supposedly failsafe device, the BOP. Accordingly, there was an enormous sense of expectation when the device, the height of a five-storey building, was brought to the surface and towed ashore, months after the accident. A huge amount of effort was devoted to trying to understand just how and why it had failed. The BOP acquired an almost mythical status. Here is how one writer described it a year later:[4]

> "[T]he critical hardware was a mile below the surface of the sea, where only remotely controlled vehicles could venture. People couldn't quite see what was going on. They literally groped in the dark. They guessed, wrongly — and people died, and the rig sank, and the oil gushed forth."

But the BOP was only the last line of defence and, arguably, not the most important. The defence metaphor is the key to a much more sophisticated understanding of this accident. The prevention of major accidents depends on defence-in-depth, that is, a series of barriers to keep hazards under control. In the drilling industry, the concept of "barrier" often refers to a physical barrier (eg a cement plug) and the usual philosophy is that there should be at least two physical barriers in place at all times to prevent a blowout. However, there is a more general and more widely used meaning of the word "barrier" that includes non-physical barriers such as training, procedures, testing, and engineering controls. Accidents occur when all of these barriers fail simultaneously. The ubiquitous Swiss cheese model developed by Professor Jim Reason conveys this idea (see Figure 1.1[5]). Each slice of cheese represents a fallible barrier, and accidents only occur when all of the holes line up.

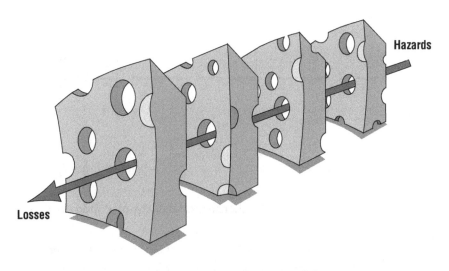

FIGURE 1.1: Swiss cheese model

This is an extremely useful way to think about accident causation, since it acknowledges and depicts the complex nature of major accidents. In particular, it enables us to think about the contribution of each and every barrier failure without falling into the trap of assuming that any one of these is *the* cause of the accident. Each is *a* cause, in the sense that, had that barrier not failed, the accident would not have occurred, but it cannot be said that any one such failure gave rise to the accident since, by itself, it clearly didn't. On this view, there is no such thing as *the* cause. Only the simultaneous failure of all of the barriers is sufficient to cause an accident.

While the Swiss cheese model is an aid to rational understanding of why accidents occur, it does not lend itself to the attribution of blame or liability. In the case of the Macondo accident, three different companies, BP, Transocean and Halliburton, had some responsibility for one or more of the failed defences. An analysis in terms of multiple failed defences means that no one company can be said to have caused the accident by its own actions or inactions. Lawyers in the blowout litigation will be seeking to paint one party or another as having caused the accident. We should not expect them, therefore, to make any use of Swiss cheese thinking.

I have already alluded to the defences that failed in the Macondo incident: the failure of the cement job; the decision to dispense with cement evaluation; the misinterpretation of the well integrity test results; the failure of monitoring; and the failure of the BOP. This sequence of failures is represented in Figure 1.2.

Figure 1.2 does not depict all of the barriers that failed. Importantly, it does not depict several barriers that failed *after* the blowout. They will be identified later.

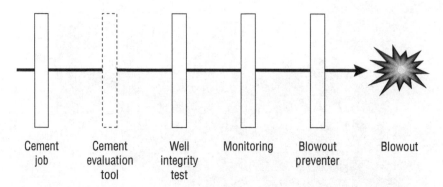

| Cement job | Cement evaluation tool | Well integrity test | Monitoring | Blowout preventer | Blowout |

FIGURE 1.2: Preliminary Swiss cheese model of the Macondo accident

Moreover, the depiction is not as detailed as it could be. Some of these defences can be decomposed into sub-defences, all of which failed. Nevertheless, the diagram is sufficient for present purposes; it is presented here so that the reader may refer back to it from time to time for orientation.

BP's own analysis of the Macondo incident, the first major analysis to appear, used the Swiss cheese imagery. Its representation of the accident is reproduced as Figure 1.3.[6] The details of this diagram are unimportant at this stage.

BP's analysis confined itself to identifying the barriers that had failed. It did not address the question of why they had failed, and for this, it was roundly criticised. This highlights one of the limitations of the simple Swiss cheese model depicted above: it does not account for barrier failure. A more complex version of the Reason model is shown in Figure 1.4.[7] The top of the diagram shows the Swiss cheese itself, with the holes all lined up. Beneath that is a triangle which suggests that the immediate causes of these barrier failures may be unsafe acts by individuals, which are the result of local workplace factors, which in turn are a consequence of organisational factors. The thick arrows leading upwards represent this causal sequence. The "latent condition pathways" at the left of the diagram are a recognition that local workplace and organisational factors may result in barrier failures independently of the actions, safe or otherwise, of frontline workers.* The thick arrows leading downwards represent the direction of causal investigation, aiming to get to what Reason sees as the bedrock causes of accidents. The diagram could and should be extended to identify factors at the level of government regulation as well.[8]

The analysis in this book is inspired by this more complex view of accident causation. It identifies a series of critical defences that failed, but it goes on to ask

---

* The space shuttle accidents exemplify this possibility. No unsafe acts by shuttle crews contributed to these accidents.

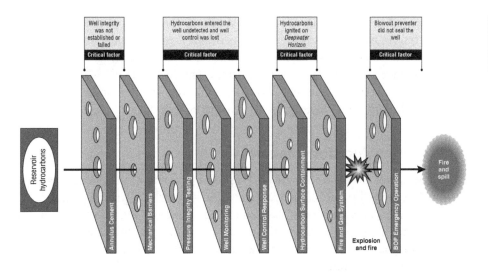

FIGURE 1.3: BP's Swiss cheese model of the Macondo accident

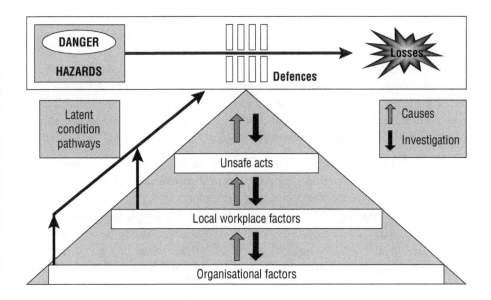

FIGURE 1.4: A more complex accident causation model

why they failed and it seeks answers primarily in the structure and functioning of BP. Among the causes to be highlighted are: a misdirected bonus system; a decentralised organisational structure; a one-sided understanding of safety; and a lack of understanding of defence-in-depth. The focus on BP is not intended as a judgment about culpability; it is simply that this is where some of the most important lessons for accident prevention are to be found.

Engineering decision-making

Major accidents occur as a result of decisions by people at many organisational levels. Decisions by people at the front line — such as plant operators and pilots — are usually the first to be pinpointed. Decisions by middle and upper-level managers are also implicated. Indeed, contemporary thinking often traces accidents back to the actions and inactions of CEOs. For example, one of the major inquiries that followed BP's 2005 Texas City Refinery disaster highlighted leadership failure by the company's CEO as a contributing factor.[9] This book does not seek to follow the trail systematically to the very top of the corporation, partly because the public inquiries did not produce any new information on this topic, but also because I have already written about this extensively in Chapter 11 of my book on the Texas City Refinery disaster, *Failure to Learn*.[10] The critical role of top leaders in accident prevention cannot, however, be overstated. It is they who must learn from major accidents and, unless they do, nothing can be expected to change.

There is one group of decision-makers that has received rather less attention in accident investigations: office-based engineers. Their decisions can and do contribute to major accidents, but this contribution is less well known. The Macondo incident provides an unusual opportunity to explore this contribution. The design decisions by BP's office-based engineers were a focus of attention in all of the inquiries, and the engineering decision-making process was laid bare in an almost unprecedented way. It is therefore a major theme in this book.

Even though people at many levels contribute to accidents, it is often easiest to deal first with the errors of frontline employees and then identify a series of workplace and organisational factors that influenced that behaviour (in much the same way as that depicted in Figure 1.4). The contribution of other people is identified as this analysis progresses. My previous book on the Texas City Refinery disaster followed that model. In contrast, this book starts with the engineers, since it was their flawed decision-making that initiated the chain of barrier failures that led to the disaster. Chapter 2 will examine their thinking in some detail. Only in Chapters 3 and 4 will we get to the errors and mistakes by frontline employees.

Engineers are accustomed to constructing decision trees to assist in decision-making in complex environments. The Macondo engineers constructed such a tree, which came to light at one of the inquiries. It is a difficult document to decipher, but it repays close study. It turns out to be a gem, providing a fascinating insight into the thinking of the Macondo engineers, and once deciphered, it offers a vivid picture of the limitations of their decision-making process. I refer to it in more than one chapter, so it is reproduced in Appendix 1 for easy access.

Chapter outline

Chapter 2 deals with the decision-making processes of the engineers who designed the cement job that was intended to seal the bottom of the well. It shows that they took what they thought were commercial risks, without realising that they were also safety risks. Moreover, they considered only one way in which the job might fail, ignoring other possible failure modes. This was a case of collective tunnel vision.

Chapter 3 concerns the well integrity test. The results of the test clearly showed that the well was not sealed, but those carrying out the test mistakenly concluded that it was. They believed that the cement job had been successful and so they couldn't accept a result that suggested otherwise. The chapter discusses the powerful confirmation bias that overwhelmed them, and identifies various other social psychological processes that enabled them to conclude that the well was safe.

Chapter 4 looks at the remaining defence failures, including the failure of monitoring and the failure of the BOP before the blowout, and the failure of the fire prevention and the spill response systems after the blowout. It shows how these defences were all interconnected. Some were undermined by the belief that earlier defences had worked, while some relied on the proper functioning of others and did not function effectively when the earlier defences failed. The image that comes most readily to mind is falling dominos. Once one fell, all of the others collapsed. The chapter also identifies some of the problems with BP's risk assessment process.

Chapter 5 makes the now well-known distinction between process and personal safety. The importance of this distinction was underlined by the Texas City Refinery disaster in which BP failed to give proper emphasis to process safety. The chapter shows that, five years on, BP drilling operations were still primarily focused on personal safety, at the expense of process safety.

Chapter 6 identifies one of the reasons for the failure to focus on process safety, which had to do with the way safety was measured and rewarded. The performance agreements for senior BP managers included measures of personal safety, but not process safety, at least not until 2010. In that year, a measure of process safety — losses of containment — was included in performance agreements for the first time. This was a commendable development. The only problem was that this measure was not relevant to the most significant major accident event in drilling, namely, blowout. The chapter argues that process safety measures need to be chosen so that they effectively focus attention on how well relevant hazards are being managed. If such indicators are then included in performance agreements, real improvements can be expected.

Chapter 7 examines BP's organisational structure and shows how it systematically undermined engineering excellence. The Macondo engineers were answerable to local operational managers, which led them to focus on cost-cutting and speed of drilling, rather than on engineering excellence. To overcome this problem, engineers need to be made accountable to higher-level engineering managers, and this line of engineering accountability must run to the top of the organisation. BP has instituted such an arrangement for drilling operations since the Gulf of Mexico accident. The need for strong, so-called "functional" lines was identified following the Texas City Refinery accident, but it was only after the Macondo accident that BP took this lesson to heart.

Chapter 8 concerns learning from previous accidents and incidents. Most companies do this badly. The Texas City Refinery disaster would not have happened if BP had learned from previous accidents, its own and others. Its failure to learn was so dramatic that I titled my book about that accident just that — *Failure to Learn*. BP did learn from the Texas City Refinery accident but, unfortunately, not quickly enough: one of the causes of the Macondo accident was the failure to implement the lessons from Texas City fully and quickly. Transocean, too, conspicuously failed to learn from a blowout on one of its rigs just four months earlier. Had it implemented the lessons from that incident, the Macondo blowout would not have occurred.

The question of why companies fail to learn is a vexed one. Learning must be both organisational and individual. Many companies operate on the assumption that sending out one-page summaries following significant incidents is enough to ensure that the necessary learning will take place. Of course, it is not. Chapter 8 discusses some ideas about how to make learning more effective.

Chapter 9 deals with management walk-arounds, seen by some as the most effective safety activity that senior managers can undertake. It discusses a management walk-around that was taking place on the *Deepwater Horizon* on the day of the disaster, and it discusses ways in which such walk-arounds can be made more effective. It argues that, had this walk-around been better targeted, the accident might have been averted. Some readers will have seen my earlier paper on this subject.[11] For the record, Chapter 9 takes the argument in that paper a step further.

Chapter 10 is about regulation. It argues that the style of regulation in force at the time of the Macondo accident encouraged an unhealthy co-dependence between the regulator and the operators it regulated. The chapter advocates the establishment of a competent, independent regulator, enforcing safety case regulations, and it concludes that the regulatory reforms since the accident have failed to deliver this result.

Chapter 11 is a critical account of popular explanations of the Macondo incident. It deals, in particular, with the claim that BP was a particularly reckless company and the view that the accident was inevitable because of the technical complexity of what was being attempted.

Chapter 12 provides a succinct summary of the argument. Readers looking for a brief account of the human and organisational causes of the accident will find this chapter useful.

Theoretical orientation

Much of the recent literature on the causes of major accidents and ways to avoid them draws heavily on the concepts of safety culture, high reliability organisations and, most recently, resilience theory. Readers familiar with this literature may be surprised to find relatively little reference to it here. I have drawn on some of these ideas when they illuminate, but I have not wanted to be constrained by them. My aim has been to tell the Macondo story in a way that yields as many insights as possible into the causes of this tragedy.

James Reason once told me, half-jokingly, that the problem with my work was that I had not yet transcended my disciplinary origins in sociology.* I plead guilty. This is a work of sociology, drawing at times explicitly and at times implicitly on the many and varied insights of that tradition. Sociology is about humans in groups. Among other things, it is about the organisational structures and cultures that humans collectively create, and about how these in turn shape the behaviour and the ideas of individuals.** That is the subject of this book.

---

* The trajectory by which Reason transcended his own disciplinary origins in psychology can be seen in his books. *Human error*, published in 1990, is primarily a study of the psychology of human error. However, the penultimate chapter is titled "Latent errors and system disasters". This provides a transition to his 1997 book, *Managing the risks of organisational accidents*, which is an organisational, rather than a psychological, analysis.

** That is, it is about structure and agency. There is a huge literature on this topic. For a good start, see Hayes, 1994.

Endnotes

1   *Wall Street Journal*, 12 March 2012.
2   CAIB, 2003; Vaughan, 1996.
3   This is nicely demonstrated in Snook, 2000, pp 75, 206.
4   Achenbach, 2011, p 3.
5   Adapted from Reason, 2000.
6   BP, 2010, p 32.
7   Source: Reason, 1997, p 17.
8   AcciMap models of accident causation pursue the analysis to this level (Branford et al, 2009).
9   Baker et al, 2007, p 60.
10 Hopkins, 2008.
11 Hopkins, 2011a.

CHAPTER 2

TUNNEL VISION ENGINEERING

The Macondo incident is unusual in that most of the accident reports focused heavily on decisions made by office-based engineers. This provides us with a rare opportunity to explore the role of engineers in both the creation and the prevention of disasters. There is no suggestion here that engineers bear primary responsibility for this accident. Flawed decisions by many other people were involved. Moreover, the decision-making by the Macondo engineers was influenced by a broader context that will also be examined in later chapters. But, in this chapter, the spotlight will be on the way flawed engineering decision-making contributed to the disaster. We shall see that the engineers were highly selective in the risks they attended to, displaying what can reasonably be described as tunnel vision.

The chapter talks variously about the Macondo engineers and the Macondo team, so a few words of explanation are necessary. Drilling the Macondo well was a joint effort by shore-based BP personnel and rig personnel, most of whom were employees of the rig owner, Transocean. BP was represented on the rig by a *well site leader* (actually, two, one for each 12-hour shift), known as the (BP) company man. He was both a decision-maker in his own right and a conduit for decisions made ashore. His immediate boss ashore was the *well team leader*. The shore-based team consisted of this well team leader and four engineers — an operations engineer, two drilling engineers, and an engineering team leader. References to the Macondo *engineers* are usually references to this group of four. The Macondo *team* includes, in addition to these four, the well team leader and the rig-based well site leaders. Occasionally, depending on the context, the Macondo team is taken to include the Transocean drillers.

The well had been drilled down to the oil and gas-bearing sands some 13,000 ft* below the sea floor. The drilling rig was ready to move on to its next job, and the bottom of the well had to be plugged with cement so that it could be left in a safe state. It would later be converted to a producing well, when BP had the necessary infrastructure in place. At that time, the cement plug would be drilled out so that oil and gas could flow into the well and up to the surface. In the meantime, it was to be "temporarily abandoned", in the language of the industry.

---

* From here on, imperial measures only will be used since these are the units in use in the United States.

After finishing the cement job, the Macondo team declared it to have been successful — a good cement job, indeed, "a text book job". The engineering team leader said later that the cement job met the criteria that had been established by the engineering group for deciding whether the job was successful.[1]

In fact, the cement job was a failure. It had failed to achieve "zonal isolation", to use industry language again, meaning that oil and gas were free to enter the bottom of the well and to blow out, as soon as the opportunity arose. The confident assertion that the cement job was a success was therefore a tragic error.

There were some immediate consequences of the declaration that the cement job had been a success. BP had flown contractors to the rig to be available should there be any doubts about the integrity of the cement job. The contractors were armed with a cement evaluation tool, known as a cement bond log (CBL), which could be used to pinpoint any problems with the cement. This would enable the crew to carry out remedial work, should it prove necessary. The direct cost of running the CBL was $128,000.[2] In addition, the job would have taken 12 to 18 hours[3] and, given that the rig was costing approximately $1m for every day of operations, BP had good reason to forego a CBL if it was judged to be unnecessary. Since the Macondo team had already decided that the job was successful, they were in the happy position of being able to dispense with the CBL and send the contractor team home on the next helicopter flight. This was a very visible statement of confidence in the integrity of the cement job.[4]

The declaration of success almost certainly played a part in the failure of subsequent defences. The misinterpretation of the later well integrity test is a case in point. The indications from this test were that the well was not effectively sealed at the bottom. But, because those doing the test already "knew" that the cement job was a good one, they misconstrued the evidence and concluded that the well had passed the test, when it should have been clear at the time that it had failed. This will be analysed in more detail in Chapter 3.

All this gives rise to two questions:

- How did BP engineering decisions contribute to the failure of the cement job?
- What led the engineers to declare the job a success, when in fact it had failed?

These questions will be examined separately in what follows.

The failure of the cement job

The Macondo engineers chose a particular well design (that is, a particular configuration of pipes and joints) that was cheaper and would also make it easier to begin production when the time came. However, this design also made it more difficult to achieve a good cement job.[5] They would be restricted to using a relatively small quantity of cement, which reduced the margin for error; they would need to pump the cement down the well at a slower than optimal rate; and they would need to use a lighter than normal cement, foam cement, that was relatively unstable.[6] These difficulties were so serious that, at the last minute, the team considered changing to a more reliable but also more expensive well design. In the end, they stuck with the original design.[7] Apart from these design decisions, there were some other last-minute engineering decisions that also increased the risk of cement failure.[8]

The Presidential Commission was unable to establish the precise mechanism of the cement failure, but it did conclude that it was some combination of the risk factors identified above.[9] In short, the decisions by the Macondo engineers to accept these various risks contributed to the cement failure. Had they gone with the less risky but more expensive well design, the cementing difficulties mentioned above would not have arisen and the cement would almost certainly not have failed.[10]

The engineers recognised that the decisions they were taking increased the risk of cement failure.[11] For instance, here is what one of them wrote in an email about one of the risks they accepted: "[The well team leader] is right on the risk/reward equation."[12] Another engineer wrote: "But who cares, it's done, end of story, [we] will probably be fine and we'll get a good cement job."[13] These statements were much quoted in commentary after the accident, and the latter was highlighted at the beginning of Chapter 4 of the report of the Presidential Commission.

These emails appear to display a cavalier attitude to safety. They can easily be construed as suggesting that the engineers were consciously sacrificing safety to achieve cost savings. But it would be wrong to interpret them in this way, as some others have done. To understand why requires a consideration of the meaning of "risk" for BP.

The dominant meaning of risk

In the dominant discourse at BP, it was *good* to take risks. Here are the words of the head of BP's exploration and production segment, Andy Inglis, written in 2007:[14]

> "... BP operate[s] on the frontiers of the energy industry — geographically, technically and in terms of business partnerships. Challenges and risks are our daily bread ... Companies like BP increasingly work in extreme weather conditions, in increasingly deep water and in complex rock formations ... There are five key advantages [of being an international oil company]. First, taking major risks; second, assembling large and diversified portfolios; third, building deep intellectual and technical capability; fourth,

> making best use of global integration; and finally, forging long-term, mutually beneficial, partnerships ... So, first, risk. As a leading international oil company, we take and manage big risks for commensurate rewards. We take exploration risks, capital risks and ongoing operations risks ..."

This passage is a celebration of risk. Perhaps the key claim is that "we take and manage big risks for commensurate rewards". But it is immediately clear that it is one kind of risk that is being celebrated — commercial risk. Inglis is not advocating that BP take *safety* risks in order to secure financial rewards.

Inglis' thinking was highly influential, and it pervaded the Macondo drilling group, as the risk/reward comment suggests. In all of the various well design decisions that were taken by the Macondo engineers, the concept of risk that was uppermost in their minds was commercial, not safety, risk. They recognised that they were taking commercial risks but none of them ever thought that their decisions might introduce safety risks. In summary, the Macondo team was doing, at its level, exactly what was being extolled at the top of the company.

What, then, was the commercial risk? The engineers knew that, if the cement job failed, they would need to embark on a time-consuming and therefore expensive re-cementing process, known as "perforate and squeeze". This involved making holes in the side of the casing at the bottom of the well and squeezing cement through the holes. This was not just a theoretical possibility; the Macondo team had already done two remedial cement jobs higher up the well.[15] The engineers, therefore, were taking something of a gamble: if the job succeeded, they would save millions of dollars; if it failed, it would cost millions of dollars. This was a purely commercial risk, as far as they were concerned.

Losing sight of safety risk

The problem is that, when people focus on commercial risk, they can lose sight of safety risk. One of the most striking ways in which the Macondo team lost sight of safety risk was in the risk assessments that they did prior to the drilling of each well. In 2009, when the Macondo well was being planned, they were required to make a "risk register" that included both a listing of risks and their associated mitigations. The risks that were supposed to be considered included safety, environmental, scheduling, production, and cost risks. However, the risk register that was compiled for the Macondo well made no mention of any safety risks. It addressed various technical risks and, as the report of the Chief Counsel for the Presidential Commission notes, "it focused exclusively on the impact [these] risks might have on time and cost".[16] In short, the development of a risk register for the Macondo well was not a *safety* risk management process.

The interaction of safety and commercial risk

What seems to have happened for the Macondo team was that a distinction was made between commercial and safety risk, after which safety risk dropped off the agenda. The fact is, however, that accepting a commercial risk can also entail accepting a safety risk. This is something that the Macondo team did not recognise. A crucial assumption on which their thinking depended was that, if the cement job failed, they would *know* it had failed, and they would then carry out the necessary remedial work. But suppose they didn't recognise that the cement job had failed. There would then be an increased risk of a blowout and a commercial risk would have become a safety risk. The fact is that the engineers *didn't* recognise that the Macondo cement job had failed — worse still, they declared it a success — for reasons to be discussed shortly. This undermined all subsequent integrity assurance activities. In this way, what was thought to be no more than a commercial risk became a safety risk, with devastating consequences.

The question that arises at this point is whether it was reasonable for the Macondo engineers to take what they saw as purely a commercial decision to choose an option with a higher risk of failure. Their decision depended on the assumption that subsequent monitoring would be done competently and would identify any failure. Was it reasonable for them to make that assumption? Some knowledgeable commentators believe so.[17] However, a study by the regulator "identified cementing problems as one of the most significant factors leading to blowouts between 1992 and 2006" in the Gulf of Mexico.[18] This finding suggests that companies are not good at recognising cement failures. It follows that they should seek to minimise the risk of failure in the first place, and not simply rely on subsequent detection.*

There is also an important policy/philosophical issue here. The idea of defence-in-depth requires that the effectiveness of every defence should be maximised. A good cement job is one of the crucial defences against a blowout. To knowingly accept a higher than necessary risk of cement failure, and to rely on subsequent defences to detect such a failure, undermines the idea of defence-in-depth. In other words, in this situation, minimising safety risk requires that commercial risk also be minimised. This conclusion may not be universally applicable, but it is certainly one that companies, and regulators, should consider carefully.

---

* Another company I discussed these issues with told me that their default assumption is that the cement will have failed and that it is therefore necessary to carry out a CBL to evaluate the cement quality, as a matter of routine. On one occasion, the CBL revealed that the cement job had failed. They therefore carried out remedial work, squeezing more cement into the annulus. A subsequent CBL yielded equivocal results and they therefore decided to do further remediation work. Their non-operating venture partner thought that this was unnecessary, but the operating company insisted. The annulus did accept more cement at this second attempt, which the company took as a vindication of their cautious approach. Had they not been cautious, a commercial risk could easily have become a safety risk.

The failure to distinguish clearly between commercial and safety risk, and to recognise how they might interact, led to some curious interchanges at one of the inquiries. One interchange is worth examining for the confusion it demonstrates in the minds of both the questioner and the witness. The questioner had identified a series of "risk-based decisions" that were made by the Macondo engineers in the days before the blowout. The first related to "centralisers" (one doesn't need to know about centralisers to make sense of the following interchange):[19]

> Q: Did BP make a risk-based decision on running the casing with only six centralisers?
>
> A: Yes sir.
>
> Q: Which option was safer: running with 21 or 6?
>
> A: I don't think there was — in my personal opinion, either was OK.

The second answer seems to contradict the first. The explanation is that the questioner and the witness have different conceptions of risk in mind. In the first question, the questioner is thinking of safety risk, while the witness answers in terms of commercial risk. The second question is explicitly about safety risk, so now the witness denies that there were any risk implications. A similar confusion runs through the discussion of every risk-based decision in the list.

At another stage in the inquiry, the questioner tried to get a witness to consider whether the various "risk-based decisions" affected the level of "workplace safety". In each case, the witness had great difficulty answering because it was not clear to him how commercial risk decisions might impact on safety risk.[20] Take the following interchange:

> Q: Would performing a cement bond log [CBL] reduce the level of risk to workplace safety?
>
> A: I don't know.

This is a telling admission. A CBL is a test that would have given some indication of whether the cement job had been successful. Failure to perform this test increased the risk that BP would fail to recognise a defective cement job. In short, failure to perform a CBL increased the risk of a blowout and hence the risk to workplace safety. The inability of the witness to make this connection shows just how far safety risk was from the minds of decision-makers.[21] The reasons for this singular lack of attention to safety risk will be analysed in later chapters.

The declaration of success

The Macondo engineers took decisions that they knew would increase the risk of cement failure. They viewed these decisions as legitimate because, in their minds, the risk was purely commercial. What happened next is that they declared the job a success when in fact it was a failure. How could this have happened? I shall argue that there were at least four ways in which the cement job could have failed, but the engineers considered only one, and it was on this basis that they declared the job a success.[22]

To develop the argument requires some more detail about the cementing process. Figure 2.1 shows the situation prior to cementing. At this stage, the well and the steel casing are full of heavy drilling fluid, called "mud", that prevents oil and gas from flowing upwards from the "pay zone" (another industry term). Some of this mud will be removed before the rig moves on to its next assignment, thus reducing the downward pressure in the well. Oil and gas could then potentially flow to the surface either inside or outside the steel casing, unless both of these routes are blocked with cement.

In order to block the flow paths, cement is pumped down the steel casing as indicated in Figure 2.2. On arrival at the bottom, it turns the corner and flows up the annulus (the gap between the steel casing and the wall of the well). The final intended location of the cement is shown in Figure 2.3.

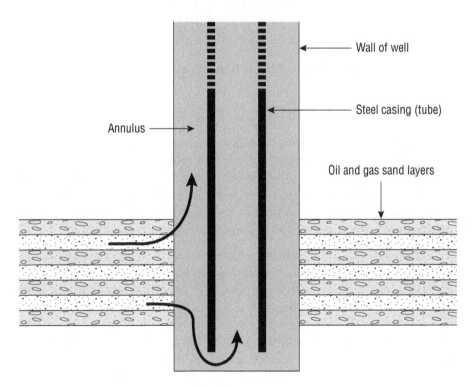

FIGURE 2.1: Escape paths for oil and gas

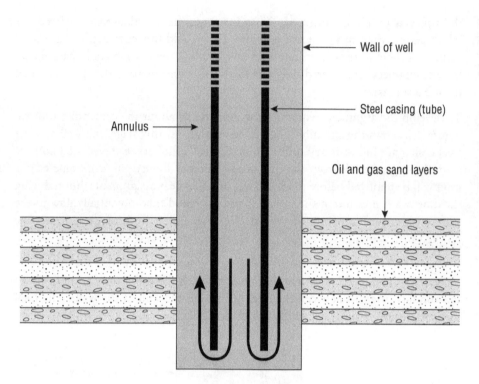

FIGURE 2.2: Path of cement being pumped

Drilling operations require a constant circulation of drilling fluid. At this stage of the operation, the circulation was down the inside of the casing and up the annulus. The cement was inserted into the flow, which meant that, as the cement was pumped down, there was mud ahead of it and mud behind it. All going well, while the cement is being pumped down and into position, as much fluid should be coming out of the top of the annulus as is going down into the casing. When this happens, the situation is described as achieving "full returns" (of fluid).

The chosen well design meant that the cement would be at very high pressure as it neared the bottom of the well. This increased the likelihood that some of the mud, or worse, some of the cement, might disappear into the oil and gas sand layers. This was the Macondo team's biggest fear because, if this happened, the cement job might not achieve zonal isolation. This possibility had been foreseen in the original risk assessment before drilling began, and the risk mitigation selected at that time was to use a "fit for purpose cementing design" with low flow rates to keep the pressure as low as possible.

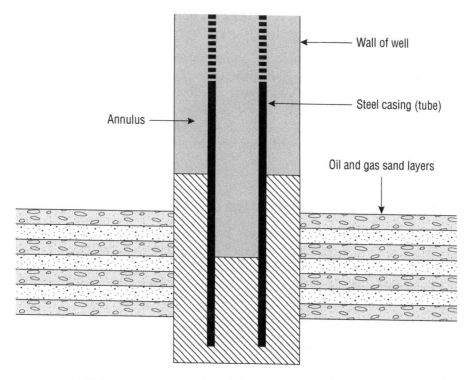

Wall of well

Steel casing (tube)

Annulus

Oil and gas sand layers

FIGURE 2.3: Final intended location of cement (diagonals)

If, despite their best efforts, some of the mud or cement did disappear into the oil and gas sands, then full returns would not occur back at the surface. In other words, if losses occurred, this would be known, and remedial action could be undertaken. On the other hand, if full returns were experienced at the surface, it could be concluded that the cement had arrived at its intended location. Full returns at the surface was thus a crucial indicator of whether or not the cement had been pumped into position.

On completion of the job, it appeared that full returns had indeed been achieved, and everyone heaved a collective sigh of relief.[23] One of the engineers emailed the team as follows: "Just wanted to let everyone know the cement job went well." He followed up with another email in which he said that the "cement team ... did a great job". One of the more senior managers then congratulated the Macondo team, writing, "Great job guys!"[24] One can almost hear the euphoria! Accordingly, a diagnostic test on the cement was deemed unnecessary and the CBL was dispensed with.

But, as we now know, the euphoria was premature. The cement job had failed. How did the Macondo team get it so wrong? What was the flaw in their thinking?

The problem was that the team drew a broader conclusion than was warranted by the evidence. As one of the engineers said later: "Everyone agreed that getting the cement in place would give us adequate zonal isolation." Here was the fallacy. The cement could be in position *and yet fail for other reasons*. The engineers were quite aware of these other failure modes but, for various reasons, they discounted them as possibilities. In the following sections, we examine their thinking in more detail.

The possibility of foam cement instability

Consider, first, the nature of the cement. Just prior to pumping, the cement slurry was mixed with nitrogen gas to create a lighter-weight foam cement. The Chief Counsel concluded that it was very likely that this foam was unstable and that the tiny bubbles of nitrogen coalesced, making the foam excessively porous and allowing hydrocarbons to pass through. In the worst case, nitrogen "breakout" could have left the cement with large gas-filled voids.[25]

The cement mixture was designed and supposedly tested by Halliburton, one of the largest service companies in the business. Halliburton was also responsible for pumping the cement on the rig. But it was BP's decision to use nitrified cement to deal with the cementing problems caused by their chosen well design.

It emerged subsequently that Halliburton was having difficulty developing a stable foam cement. Various experimental batches had proved unstable. The company claims that the formula finally used had passed the test, but there is considerable doubt as to whether the testing as performed was relevant to the conditions that pertained at the bottom of the Macondo well.[26] There is also considerable doubt as to whether the Halliburton cementer was aware of the final test results when he began the cement job.[27] The Chief Counsel was highly critical of Halliburton for these failures.[28] In the end, he made the following observation:[29]

> "The number and magnitude of errors that Halliburton personnel made while developing the Macondo foamed cement slurry point to clear management problems at that company."

The failures by Halliburton contributed significantly to the risk of nitrogen breakout. But let us return to the BP Macondo team. They were unaware of the difficulties that Halliburton was having developing an appropriate cement formula for the job. However, they knew that the foam cement posed "significant stability challenges".[30] The BP man on the rig apparently warned the rig crew to be careful with the foam cement and to be ready to shut in the well if necessary.[31] Moreover, one of the Macondo engineers had emailed Halliburton three weeks earlier asking for test results. He said: "… this is an important job and we need to have the data well in advance to make the correct decisions on this job."[32] This same engineer also made a recommendation to Halliburton about the cement formula which he recognised increased the "risk of having issues with the nitrogen". The engineering team, then, was well aware of this potential failure mode (that is, the way in which the job could fail).

The requested Halliburton test results had not arrived by the time the Macondo team was ready to go ahead with the cementing. BP had its own in-house cementing expert, so it would have been able to evaluate the test results in a knowledgeable way. But this no longer seemed to be a matter of concern, and the team authorised the cementing without ever reviewing the cement design. BP's engineering drilling manager said later that he would have expected his engineers not to have started the cement job without seeing successful test results.[33] In the end, then, the Macondo team lost sight entirely of this failure mode.

Channelling

Another failure mode that the Macondo team overlooked in its declaration of success was the possibility of what is called "channelling". The leading surface of the cement, as it is pushed up the annulus into the required position, is pushing mud ahead of it. It can happen that cement will push past some of the mud and end up a little higher up the annulus, leaving channels of mud behind. If this happens, then, after the cement sets, there is a possibility that oil and gas may push through the mud channels and escape up the annulus. This kind of channelling is particularly likely if the casing is not properly centred in the drill hole, so that the annulus on one side of the casing is narrower than on the other side (see Figure 2.4). Under these circumstances, cement is likely to move up the wider side of the annulus, leaving channels of mud on the narrower side. Channelling can also occur even when the casing is perfectly centralised, manifesting as "viscous fingers".

To minimise the risk of channelling, centralisers are attached to the casing at intervals to keep it in the centre of the drill hole. The initial design called for six centralisers.

BP was using a complex mathematical model provided by Halliburton to integrate information about pressures, pumping rates, well dimensions, position of centralisers etc, so as to come up with predictions about the success of the cement job. This model predicted that, with six centralisers, there would be severe channelling and "severe gas flow problems" up the annulus. The Halliburton modeller pointed this out to the Macondo engineering team.[34] They therefore located additional centralisers, but ultimately decided that these were not of the right type[35] and that

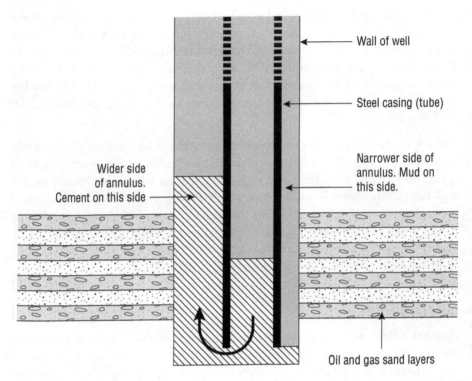

FIGURE 2.4: Channelling

it would be better to make do with the original six. Theoretically, they could have waited for more centralisers to be found and sent out to the rig, but this possibility seemed not to occur to anyone. This would have constituted an unacceptable delay. The view was that some minor adjustments to the positioning of the six centralisers would deal with the potential channelling and that it was reasonable to go ahead on this basis. They did not ask for the model to be recalculated with the centralisers repositioned to see what difference this in fact made.

The attitude of the Macondo engineers in this matter seems, on the face of it, quite reckless. How are we to understand this apparent disregard for the possibility of "severe gas flow problems"? The answer lies in the model. One of its predictions was that, if there was channelling, there would be losses into the oil and gas sands. (There is no need to go into the reasoning here.) Hence, if the cement job was carried out with no loss of returns, they could infer that there had been no channelling. Ironically, many of those involved had reason to doubt this particular model prediction, because they had personally experienced situations where there had been no loss of returns and yet channelling had occurred.[36] The Halliburton modeller said subsequently that the only way to be sure whether channelling had occurred was to use the CBL.[37] But the Macondo engineering team accepted the model prediction unquestioningly. What made this all the more remarkable is that several of those who accepted the model predictions in this matter had, in other circumstances, expressed doubt about the accuracy of the model and its predictions. The pattern seemed to be that, when the model gave results that were consistent with what they wanted to do, they accepted those results, but when the model results proved awkward, they either disregarded them or found a way to update the model with more accurate or more recent information that gave them the results they wanted.[38]

This is an example of the well-known confirmation bias that bedevils human decision-making. Even though this bias can sometimes appear conscious or intentional, psychologists insist that this is not necessarily the case. In other words, it cannot be assumed that the engineers were aware of just how selectively they were using the model. Confirmation bias was even more apparent in later well integrity tests, and will be discussed in more detail in Chapter 3.

The upshot was that the Macondo engineers discounted the need to pay particular attention to the possibility that the cement job might fail as a result of channelling. This was a failure mode that they could basically ignore, on the assumption that the model predictions were accurate — an assumption that they were not prepared to make in other circumstances.

BP claimed that it was unlikely that this failure mode contributed to the cement failure, but the Commission took issue with this conclusion and argued that channelling "could very well have damaged the integrity of the cement in the annular space".[39] But the issue of whether it did or didn't contribute to the failure is not relevant here. The point is that this was a potential failure mode to which the Macondo engineers paid scant attention.

Contamination

The third failure mode that was effectively ignored by the Macondo engineers was the possibility that the cement might be contaminated with mud on its long journey down the casing. If this happened, it could compromise the ability of the cement to set.[40] There were several reasons to expect that this might be a problem and the Macondo team discussed this at one of their planning meetings. According to the engineering team leader, he wanted "to make sure everybody was comfortable with the cement volumes and the like, and part of that was based off of the contamination issues".[41] He went on, "everyone that walked out of that room thought the job that we had come up with was adequate for the execution".[42] The Chief Counsel argued that the cement may well have failed as a result of contamination.[43] But, again, whether it did or didn't is beside the point here. This was a failure mode that the

Macondo team did not take into account when making their announcement that the cement job was a success.

Some reflections

Let us take stock at this point. Long before the cement job was actually carried out, the Macondo engineers were aware, to varying degrees, of at least four possible ways in which the cement job might fail to achieve zonal isolation:

(1) loss of cement into the oil and gas sands;

(2) instability of the nitrogen foam cement;

(3) channelling in the annulus; and

(4) contamination.

The cement job was designed to take all of these things into account. If the job went as planned, they should get effective zonal isolation. They knew that they could not simply assume that all would go as planned and that they would need some evidence to that effect. But the only evidence they sought was in relation to the first potential failure mode.[44] They did not seek direct evidence in relation to the latter three modes, and implicitly assumed that they could rely on the various design decisions and assumptions they had made to deal with these possibilities. To announce that the cement job had been a success in these circumstances was going beyond the evidence. They had unwittingly created an evidentiary gap which turned into an evidentiary trap.

The Macondo engineers displayed tunnel vision. They had their eyes set on a particular goal — a well design that was cheaper and would make production easier when the time came. They were very aware of *one* risk associated with this design, namely, that, in the process of cementing the casing, they would lose cement into the oil and gas sands. Accordingly, they took a number of decisions to minimise this risk without giving sufficient consideration to the additional risks that were introduced by these decisions. These additional risks were somehow peripheral in their minds. It all came down to one simple test: did they get full returns or didn't they?[45] The tunnel vision of the Macondo engineers seemed to eliminate their peripheral risk awareness almost entirely.

It is worth reminding ourselves at this point of one of the characteristics of high reliability organisations (HROs) — *reluctance to simplify*. I draw on the words of Weick and Sutcliffe:[46]

> "Success in any coordinated activity requires that people simplify in order to stay focused on a handful of key issues and key indicators."

That is clearly what the Macondo engineers were doing:

> "[But] HROs take deliberate steps to create more complete and nuanced pictures. They simplify less and see more. Knowing that the world they face is complex, unstable, unknowable, and unpredictable, they position themselves to see as much as possible."

That is not what the Macondo engineers were doing.

It is, of course, no use urging organisations to become more like HROs. There are structural reasons why some organisations approach this ideal more closely than others. Later chapters will deal with some of the organisational reasons why the behaviour of the Macondo engineers was so far from the HRO ideal.

We can put all this in more conventional risk management terms. The original risk register, drawn up before the well was started, identified the possibility that the cement job might not achieve "zonal isolation". Notice that, at this point, the risk is broadly stated and does not assume any particular failure mode. But when the mitigation is specified, it is clear that the team has only one failure mode in mind — losses into the oil and gas sands — because the mitigation that is identified is to use a "fit for purpose cementing design" "with low circulating rates", all to keep the pressure as low as possible. The whole purpose is to avoid forcing cement out into the oil and gas sands. But — and this is the critical point — this mitigation was not itself formally risk assessed. Had it been, the team might have had to formally acknowledge that the mitigation introduced additional risks which also needed to be carefully managed. Risk assessment procedures all too often specify mitigations that are ineffective for various reasons. But what happened here went beyond this: the mitigation strategy itself introduced new risks.

The problem is even clearer in a document prepared just five days before the blowout. The document was produced as part of BP's "management of change" (MoC) process and was designed to provide formal authorisation for the well design that was finally chosen.[47] It noted that there had been two earlier events in this section of the well in which mud had been lost into the surrounding sands. This risk was therefore uppermost in everyone's mind. As a result, the risk that had been identified in the earlier document as failure to achieve "zonal isolation" became, in the MoC document, much more specifically, "lost circulation during the cement job", meaning loss of cement into the oil and gas sands. In other words, from the outset, the MoC document contemplated only one of the four possible failure modes identified above.

The document then went on to specify the mitigation:

> "The cement job has been designed to minimise the ... [pressure] as low as practical: foam cement, light weight spacer, and a small base of

oil spacer, along with low pump rates, will be used together to keep
... [the pressure] below an acceptable level."

As already noted, this mitigation strategy introduced additional risks, without any
acknowledgment or formal recognition.

Interestingly, the team did consider one or two other risks that potentially affected
the integrity of the well in the longer term, that is, during its production phase. At
least one of these risks had previously resulted in the destruction of a producing
well, and BP was especially sensitive to this possibility.[48] But these additional risks
had nothing to do with the cementing job and its ability to achieve zonal isolation.
In relation to those matters, BP's engineers had very little risk awareness beyond the
primary risk that stood in the way of a successful job, namely, cement losses into
the oil and gas sands.

Last-minute anomalies

There were some last-minute anomalies that demonstrated the single-minded
focus of the Macondo team on getting the job finished. Before cementing began,
the rig crew needed to activate a valve at the bottom of the casing (not shown
in the diagrams in this chapter). To activate the valve, they needed to increase the
pump pressure until it generated a pressure differential across the value of between
500 and 700 psi (pounds per square inch). The activation did not occur at this
pressure and so the crew increased the pressure, gingerly, incrementally, until finally,
at 3,410 psi, roughly six times the expected pressure, something gave way and the
pressure dropped. No one was sure what had happened. An engineer on site at
the time emailed, saying: "... we blew it at 3,140, still not sure what we blew
yet." The well site leader said: "I'm afraid we've blown something higher up in the
casing string." Another engineer wrote: "... shifted at 3,140 psi. Or we hope so."[49]
Despite these doubts, the team proceeded on the assumption that the valve had
been activated as planned. The Chief Counsel concluded that there was a significant
possibility that the valve had not in fact activated and that the pressure drop was
caused by something else.[50] This would have significantly increased the risk that the
cement might fail to isolate the pay zone.[51]

There was a further anomaly. After the presumed activation had occurred, the
pressure required to keep the mud moving was much lower than expected —
another sign that something might be wrong.[52] The Macondo engineers were at
a loss to explain this, and eventually they concluded, without other evidence, that
the pressure gauge was probably broken.[53] They were perturbed by the anomaly,
but they felt comfortable proceeding, they said, because they knew that the cement
would be pressure tested later.[54] (I shall return to the significance of this assumption
in Chapter 4.)

These anomalies indicated that things had not gone to plan. They were warnings that something might be wrong. Had the Macondo engineers paid heed to these warnings, there were steps they might have taken to deal with the problem.[55] But they didn't. They pressed on towards their goal, hoping that somehow it would all turn out for the best. One might have thought that these anomalies would have made them a little more cautious about declaring the success of the cement job when they did, but that was not to be.

This is not the way that HROs behave, to refer again to that literature. According to Weick and Sutcliffe, HROs:[56]

> "… are *preoccupied with their failures*, large and mostly small. They treat any lapse as a symptom that something is wrong with the system, something that could have severe consequences if separate small errors happened to coincide at one awful moment … Anomalies are noticed when they are still tractable and can still be isolated."

The Macondo engineers were not willing to stop and consider these anomalies carefully and to modify their activity to take account of the increased uncertainty. They were on the home stretch and were keen to finish a job that was very much behind schedule. These were circumstances that minimised their sensitivity to risk and undermined their capacity for HRO functioning.

Consensus decision-making

The fact that the Macondo engineering group made poor decisions is, in part, attributable to the decision-making mechanisms they used. What I want to show in this section is that decision-making tended to be by consensus, which meant that no one took real responsibility.

For example, the decision not to run a CBL was taken at a team meeting. The well team leader said to the group: "Does anyone see the need for running the bond log?"[57] No one did. According to a previously agreed decision tree, it was unnecessary to run a CBL because they had achieved full returns. This was formally the basis on which the decision was taken, but the reality was that the well team leader acted only after consensus had been established. He confirmed later that, in his view, the decision was made by consensus.[58]

Let us reflect on this for a moment. Of course, it is appropriate to consult before making a decision to ensure that the decision-making is as informed as possible. But what happened here is that a meeting held to gather opinions became, in fact, a decision-making meeting. There are two problems with this kind of decision-making. First, everyone is responsible for the decision which means, in turn, that no one person feels personally responsible. The end result, in other words, is non-responsible decision-making. The second problem is that the decision depends on the precise membership of the group. It is conceivable that, had certain other people been present or certain of those present absent, the decision might have been different. It has been noted that hazard identification exercises, such as HAZOPs, can depend critically on whether or not people with operational experience are present, in short, that the composition of the HAZOP or hazard identification team is critical. Consensus decision-making is inherently problematic in this way.

Many important engineering decisions for the Macondo well seem to have been made in this casual, consensus-seeking way. In one documented case, one of the engineers, who happened to be on the rig at the time, emailed the team ashore as follows:

> "Recommendation out here is to displace to seawater at 8,300, then set the cement plug. Does anyone have any issues with this?"

One shore-based engineer replied: "Seems OK to me."[59]

It is interesting to think about what is going on here. The recommendation has far-reaching implications (not discussed here). The engineer on the rig is seeking consensus among the email recipients. Only one replies. We know that the non-response of others was treated as agreement because the recommendation was, in fact, implemented. However, another engineer said later that the team never discussed this issue. One can easily see why this was his perception.

A word that comes up again and again in the context of this consensus decision-making is "comfortable". As noted earlier, the engineering team leader wanted "to make sure everybody was comfortable with the cement volume". In another context, a witness said that "all parties need to be comfortable"[60] with a decision. But comfort is well short of active agreement. This is hardly an adequate basis for making important technical decisions. No one feels accountable when decisions are made in this way. No one's head will be on the chopping block if something goes wrong.

Of course, BP did have the more formal decision-making process mentioned earlier — the "management of change" (MoC) process. It required a long string of signatures. The MoC document on the final well design, for example, was initiated by one engineer, verified by a second, subject to technical review by three others, and then approved by two further people. This chain of scrutiny was intended to provide assurance about the soundness of the proposed course of action.

One might have thought that this process would lead to more careful and more responsible decision-making. It might have, if the reviewers and approvers had been truly independent of the proposer. However, the fact is that the reviewers and approvers were often involved in developing the proposal. There is an understandable logic to this. But when it comes to sign-off, it means that reviewers and approvers are not looking at the proposal with fresh eyes and may well sign off without giving the document proper attention. As a result, the system of assurance is undermined and the integrity of the whole MoC process is subverted. The Macondo engineers had unwittingly converted their MoC procedure into a consensus decision-making process, with all the pitfalls of that process.

The failures of the review and approval process as practised by the Macondo engineers are easily demonstrated. In particular, despite the string of signatures, the MoC for the final well design identified only one risk in relation to the cement job — failure of the cement to get to its intended location. Interestingly, the document had attached to it a decision tree intended to guide the team through the final stages of well construction (see Appendix 1). Not surprisingly, this tree contained the same defect.

The decision tree repays further study. It will be recalled that the team declared the cement job a success on the basis of achieving full returns. Conversely, if they had had less than full returns, they would have acknowledged that they had a problem and used a CBL to evaluate the extent of the problem. At least that was the understanding of one of the reviewers/approvers. *Yet this is not what the decision tree indicated.* In the event of less than full returns, the decision tree embarked on a convoluted path of twists and turns, all designed to *avoid* having to do a CBL. Only if all else failed did the tree envisage a CBL. This was completely at odds with the understanding of the reviewer/approver. What the tree depicted was not what he intended, but this fact had entirely escaped his attention. Apparently, it had escaped the attention of others as well.[61] It seems that the review and approval process simply failed to function on this occasion.

There is something troubling about the long trail of reviewers and approvers required by the MoC process: it diffuses responsibility for decision-making. No matter what the formal situation, the MoC process shares responsibility around, with the result that no one person feels truly responsible for the decision.

Conclusion

The Macondo team gave little or no thought to safety risk. The concept of risk for them meant commercial risk, and all of their risk assessments were aimed at identifying and mitigating commercial risk. Given this approach, it is understandable that engineering excellence was not a top priority because, in their view, if they got it wrong, they could always take remedial action. What they failed to understand was that commercial risk could entail safety risk, because the failure of the cement job would bring them one step closer to an adverse safety outcome.

But, even from the point of view of commercial risk, their risk assessments were poor. The Macondo team focused on only one of the ways in which the cement job could fail, losing sight of several other possible failure modes. When it appeared that the cement job had been successful in terms of the one failure mode that they were concerned about, they declared the job a success, when in fact it had failed.

Part of the reason for the poor decisions that the Macondo team made was the decision-making process they adopted — consensus-seeking. If all present felt "comfortable" with a proposed course of action, then the proposal was adopted. The result was that, in practice, no one person was really accountable for the decision. This was the case even when the formal MoC decision-making process was used. Verifiers and approvers were involved in the development of the proposal, rather than verifying and approving at arm's length. Moreover, the sheer number of verifiers and approvers could only serve to diffuse accountability for the final decision. Companies often talk about the need for single-point accountability, but that was far from the daily reality of the Macondo team.

In principle, the process of seeking input from team members should not be conflated with decision-making. Decisions should be made after all relevant input has been gathered, in a separate decision-making process, preferably by a single decision-maker. Only in this way can real accountability be achieved. I shall develop these ideas further in Chapter 3, which deals with decision-making failures even more dramatic than those discussed here.

The inadequacy of the decision-making process itself does not provide a fully satisfying account of the poor decisions made by the Macondo engineers. When all is said and done, it still seems puzzling that they acted and decided as they did. What is largely missing from this account is the broader context that contributed to their decisions. That context includes:

- the organisational structure of BP's engineering activity;
- the heavy focus on personal safety, as opposed to process safety; and
- the way in which economic pressures were unconstrained by other considerations.

These matters will be dealt with in later chapters. This will provide a much clearer understanding of why the Macondo engineers made the flawed decisions that they did.

Endnotes

1   DWI, 7 October, am, Walz, p 185. "DWI" refers to the transcript from the joint BOEMRE/ Coast Guard inquiry, originally available at www.deepwaterinvestigation.com. I accessed the website during the inquiry. Unfortunately, it is no longer freely available.

2   DWI, 28 August, Gagliano, pp 362, 363.

3   DWI, 7 October, pm, Guide, p 203.

4   A likely cause of cement failure was the breakout of nitrogen. A CBL would have detected nitrogen breakout, according to the Chief Counsel for the Presidential Commission (CCR, p 74). This is also Halliburton's view — see the press release of 28 October 2010, "Halliburton comments on national Commission cement testing". BP thought it "unlikely" that a CBL would have identified the problems. See its statement to the National Academy of Engineers (NAE) (BP, 2011, p 21). See also the NAE report itself, pp 21 and 28. Figure 2.5 of the NAE report shows what a CBL would have "seen".

5   CCR, p 64.

6   CCR, pp 78-81.

7   This uncertainty worried the well site leaders. One told his boss (CCR, p 61): "There [have] been so many last minute changes to the operation that the well site leaders have finally come to their wits end."

8   For example, decisions about the use of centralisers.

9   CCR, pp 96, 97, 111; see also BP, 2011, p 16.

10   Note: this problem with the long string well design needs to be distinguished from the argument, made by some observers, that a long string design is inherently more risky because it has fewer barriers in the annulus. The latter claim is not made here.

11   CCR, pp 116, 124.

12   OSC, p 97.

13   CCR, p 103.

14   A Inglis, "The role of an international oil company in the 21st century", Sanford Bernstein 4th Annual Strategic Decisions Conference, 25 September 2007. Website at www.bp.com/ genericarticle.do?categoryId=98&contentId=7037044. I am indebted for this reference to the excellent paper by W Gale, "Perspectives on changing safety culture and managing risk", Deepwater Horizon Study Group, January 2011.

15   Transocean, 2011, p 20.

16   CCR, p 245.

17   Personal communication.

18   OSC, p 99; Izon et al, 2007, pp 84-90.

19   DWI, 22 July, p 76.

20   DWI, 27 August, pp 50-53.

21   See also the confusion about applying a safety risk matrix to the cement job (DWI, 27 August, pp 29, 30).

22   This is also the conclusion in CCR, p 107.

23   According to BOEMRE (pp 56, 195), the team was misled by inaccurate sensors and full returns had not in fact been achieved. If so, this was their first mistake, worth exploring in its own right. But what is of interest in this chapter is the fact that, having satisfied themselves that they had achieved full returns, they discounted all other potential failure modes.

24 CCR, p 93.

25 CCR, p 97.

26 BP, 2011, p 14.

27 CCR, p 118

28 CCR, pp 111, 118.

29 CCR, p 123.

30 CCR, p 124.

31 DWI, 27 May, Harrell, p 72.

32 CCR, p 115.

33 DWI, 8 December, pm, Spraghe, pp 170, 171.

34 CCR, p 86. He told two of them: "Hey, I think we have a potential problem here. There's a potential for flow due to the six centralisers. I'm showing channelling." And again: "I told them of the potential for blowout." DWI, 24 August, Gagliano, pp 253, 364.

35 This understanding was wrong, but that is beside the point here.

36 DWI, 26 August, Sims, p 227; DWI, 27 August, Cocales, p 142; DWI, 7 October, Walz, p 97.

37 DWI, 24 August, Gagliano, pp 270, 335.

38 This is also the conclusion of CCR, p 106.

39 CCR, p 97.

40 CCR, p 62.

41 DWI, 7 October, pm, Walz, p 34.

42 DWI, 7 October, pm, Walz, p 35.

43 CCR, pp 93, 96.

44 This is also the view of CCR, p 107.

45 There were two other criteria mentioned — bumping the plug and rising lift pressures. But these were also tests of whether the cement had got into position, the first failure mode, and provided no information about the other three failure modes (CCR, p 107).

46 Weick & Sutcliffe, 2001, p 11.

47 CCR, p 61.

48 CCR, p 64.

49 CCR, p 89.

50 CCR, p 99.

51 CCR, p 102.

52 CCR, p 89.

53 CCR, pp 90, 106.

54 CCR, p 90.

55 CCR, pp 106, 107.

56 Weick & Sutcliffe, 2001, pp 10, 13 (emphasis in original).

57 DWI, 7 October, am, Walz, p 185.

58 DWI, 22 July, Guide, p 183.

59   CCR, p 140.

60   DWI, 8 December, am, Robinson, p 90.

61   Actually, the confusion was even worse than this. One of the engineers distributed a work plan
     that treated even *partial* returns as indicating success (CCR, p 94).

Chapter

2

CHAPTER 3

CONFIRMATION BIAS: THE WELL INTEGRITY TEST

The Macondo well was tested shortly before the blowout. The results indicated unambiguously that it was not properly sealed and that oil and gas would force their way to the top at the first opportunity. Unfortunately, those carrying out the test misinterpreted these results and concluded that the well was sealed. How could they possibly have made such a dreadful mistake? That is the question this chapter seeks to answer.

A common explanation provided in the various reports is that the people doing the test lacked the necessary competence. While true, this is an explanation that obscures more than it reveals. It invites further questions. Why were there people working on the rig who did not have the necessary competence? Why was BP unaware of this lack of competence?

Let us pursue this latter question for a moment. The fact is that it is easier for managers to *assume* competence than to *verify* it. As one senior BP executive said at interview, "You are managing a group of professionals",[1] which makes it difficult to question their competence. In fact, one of the BP employees involved in misinterpreting the evidence had just been transferred to the rig. A senior official from Transocean, the company that owned the rig, was aware that the operation was at a critical phase, and he accordingly asked BP about the new man's experience. He was told that the individual "was a very experienced, very competent well-site leader, with numerous years of experience and it wouldn't be a concern".[2] Sadly, this individual, through no fault of his own, had very little idea about how to conduct the well integrity test. BP managers simply assumed that he was competent in all aspects of the job. He was not. An independent drilling engineer commenting on this situation notes that "we can never assume competency, and if we do so, that is a high risk of the first order".[3]

Lack of competence, like human error more generally, is merely a starting point for explanation, not a satisfactory explanation in its own right. It was not just the individual recently transferred to the rig who misinterpreted the test results. Several others were involved in the decision, all of whom had many years of experience. Apparently, none of them had the necessary competence. I shall return later to why this might have been the case.

Another explanation, that BP itself identified, was that the written procedures for the test were not sufficiently detailed. Again, while this is true, it does not account for the inability of all present to recognise the unambiguous evidence of failure that confronted them.

Clearly, there were other factors at work and a more searching inquiry is necessary to identify these factors. As we shall see, a number of well-known social psychological processes contributed to the outcome. In particular, decision-making was shaped by: confirmation bias; the normalisation of deviation; inadequate situational awareness; and groupthink. These processes will all be discussed in this chapter.

The test

To begin with, we need to understand in more detail what was happening. The rig had successfully drilled down into the oil and gas-bearing sands, known as the "pay zone", 13,000 ft below the sea floor. Cement had then been pumped into position at the bottom of the well, to seal it. The drilling rig was floating on the surface of the sea and the well head was located 5,000 ft below, on the sea floor. The rig and the well head were connected by a tube, called a "riser" (see Figure 3.1). The riser and the well itself were full of a heavy drilling fluid, so-called mud, about twice the density of seawater. While ever this mud was in position, the well was "overbalanced", meaning that the pressure it exerted at the bottom of the well was enough to prevent oil and gas forcing their way to the surface. But the rig was about to depart for its next job and, before doing so, the riser and the mud it contained had to be removed. That would leave the well "underbalanced", and the cement seal at the bottom of the well would need to function as intended in order to prevent a blowout. The next step, therefore, was an integrity test to ensure that the well was indeed properly sealed.

The test involved temporarily reducing the pressure in the well to below the pressure exerted by the fluids in the pay zone, and observing what happened. If the cement seal was not working, oil and gas would force their way into the bottom of the well and the pressure in the well would rise. If the seal was good, the pressure in the well would remain at the reduced level.

The detail of what was supposed to happen is as follows. The drill pipe would be inserted into the well, down to the position shown in Figure 3.2. Seawater would then be pumped down the drill pipe under high pressure, forcing the mud above upwards, and creating the water-filled cavity seen in the diagram. The curved arrow in Figure 3.2 indicates the direction of water flow. When the upper interface[4] between water and mud arrived at the well head (or, more accurately, the blowout preventer (BOP)), a rubber seal would be closed around the drill pipe, as shown. From then on, the mud above the rubber seal would be supported by the rubber

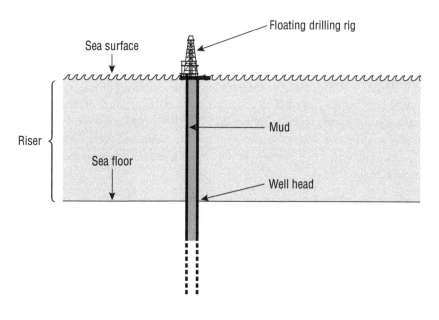

FIGURE 3.1: Riser

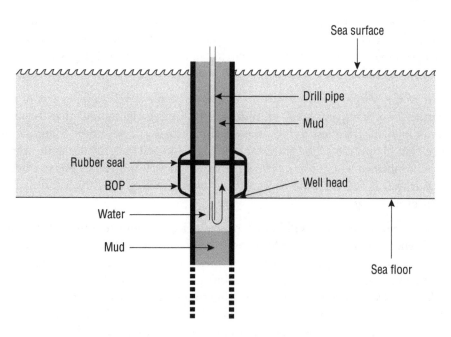

FIGURE 3.2: Seawater pumped down drill pipe

seal. Next, the valve at the top of the drill pipe on the rig would be opened, thus reducing the pressure at that point to zero. The pressure in the water-filled cavity below the rubber seal would now be equal to the pressure created by the 5,000 ft of water sitting above it in the drill pipe. As far as the well was concerned, it would be as if all that was sitting above the well head was a column of water 5,000 ft high. (Remember: the heavy mud in the riser is not exerting pressure on the water below because it is supported by the rubber seal.) In other words, the test would simulate what it would be like when the riser and mud it contained were completely gone. If all went well, when the pressure at the top of the drill pipe was reduced to zero, it would remain at zero.

Consider now what actually happened. After some preliminary adjustments,[5] the team opened the valve at the top of the drill pipe to "bleed off" water and reduce the pressure to zero. But as soon as they closed the valve, the pressure began to rise. This was a clear indication that the well had failed the test and was not in fact sealed. Tragically, the team did not draw this conclusion. Instead, they tried a second time and again the same thing happened. The well had now twice conclusively failed the test, but the decision-making group could not accept what this was telling them.

Confirmation bias

Before describing the next steps taken by the group, we need to consider why they seemed oblivious to the evidence before their eyes. The explanation is that it was inconceivable to them that the well might fail the test. This was a possibility that they simply did not contemplate.

Part of the reason for this is that it was very rare for a well to fail a test of this nature. Two "company men" on different rigs independently said that they had never known such a test to fail. In these circumstances, a powerful "confirmation bias" was in operation. The purpose of the Macondo well integrity test in the minds of all concerned was not to *investigate* whether the well was sealed, but to *confirm* that it was. It was therefore necessary to continue testing until this confirmation was forthcoming.

"Confirmation bias" is a well-known psychological phenomenon that refers to the preference people have for information that confirms, rather than disconfirms, their beliefs. It is an unconscious process, not a deliberate attempt to build a one-sided case.[6] Teams carrying out risk assessments are renowned for this kind of bias. Where a particular course of action is being considered, teams will frequently make selective use of information suggesting that the risk is acceptably low and discard or fail to consider information that suggests otherwise. Various examples of this came to light in the investigation into the Texas City Refinery accident.[7]

Confirmation bias was not confined to those carrying out the well integrity test. There is evidence that BP's shore-based engineers thought in similar terms. To develop this point requires a few words of preliminary explanation. Just a few days earlier, the engineers had developed a decision tree to guide the decision-making process in the finishing stages of well construction. (This is reproduced in Appendix 1 and the reader will need to consult Appendix 1 to understand the following discussion.) As every engineer would know, a decision box is represented in such diagrams as a diamond, with at least two outcomes emanating from the points of the diamond, depending on the answer to the question in the decision box. Several such decision boxes can be seen in the diagram in Appendix 1. A square box is used when the action is not a decision but simply one of a series of actions to be completed. Because it is not a decision, there is only one outcome arrow from such a box, pointing to the next action. There are several such action boxes in the diagram.

Consider, now, the box on the right side of the diagram immediately below the decision diamond. It contains the words "test casing". There were actually two tests involved here, one of which was the well integrity test under discussion. But notice that this is not a diamond-shaped box and there is only one outcome, which assumes that the tests are successful. One of the engineers later acknowledged that this was an omission and that test failure would launch the decision-makers down another path, not shown on the diagram. It might be suggested that this is a trivial omission from the decision tree, since everyone would understand this. However, the symbolism is significant: the diagram does not conceive of the possibility of failure!

There is one further piece of evidence that confirms this interpretation of the mindset of the engineers. Rig personnel were provided with sets of instructions each day about the activities for that day. The first draft of the work plan for the day on which the blowout occurred did not contain any reference to the well integrity test.[8] It was only when the senior Transocean manager on the rig requested that such a test be performed that this omission was rectified. It is clear that the test was not top of mind for the BP engineers. This was not seen as a vital opportunity to test the integrity of the well but, rather, an almost redundant step which would simply confirm the integrity of the well.

To return to the group carrying out the well integrity test, there was a particular circumstance that ensured that they did not approach the test with an open mind. The cement job on the well had been completed just hours earlier and engineers had declared that the cement job was a success. Strictly speaking, they were not entitled to make this claim. The evidence they had was that the cement had been successfully pumped into position, but not that it had set properly, nor that it effectively sealed the well. Nevertheless, as BP's well team leader said: "… everyone involved with the [cement] job on the rig site was completely satisfied with the job."[9] This would have powerfully reinforced the confirmation bias of the decision-makers. As BP officials said later, given the circumstances, the people engaged in the integrity test regarded it as nothing more than a box-ticking exercise.

The normalisation of warning signs — the "bladder" effect

Let us return to the thought processes of the decision-making group. They were perplexed. The testing was not going as expected. Given their belief that the well was secure, how were they to make sense of the rising pressure at the top of the drill pipe? What happened next was a classic case of the normalisation of warning signs. They managed to find an explanation for the rise that did not call into question the integrity of the well.

Before considering this explanation, we need to understand a little more about the phenomenon of normalisation. The best known account is provided by sociologist Diane Vaughan in her discussion of the space shuttle *Challenger*, which caught fire and plunged to earth in 1986, killing the seven astronauts on board.[10] The integrity of the booster rockets depended on certain rubber seals, known as O-rings. It had been discovered on several previous launches that they did not perform as required at low temperatures. Indeed, they malfunctioned. Nevertheless, they had not failed totally. Over time, this partial malfunction was reconceptualised as normal, and the risk of total failure came to be judged as acceptably low. Vaughan described this as the normalisation of deviance, by which she meant the normalisation of deviation, or partial malfunction, or increased risk. The temperature on the launch day was colder than at previous launches. But the technical malfunction had been normalised. The launch was thus given the go-ahead. This time, the seals failed totally, with catastrophic results.* Tragically, the same process contributed to the *Columbia* space shuttle accident 17 years later.[11]

The normalisation of warning signs is a variation on this theme. It is almost always the case that major accidents are preceded by events that amount to warnings, and that, had these warnings been heeded, the accident would have been averted. For instance, four men drowned in an Australian coal mine when miners inadvertently broke through into old, abandoned workings that were full of water, as old workings

---

* The best operational managers in hazardous industries are acutely aware of the phenomenon of normalisation. They know that, if one of several controls that are supposed to be in place is not working, the risk of failure may only be marginally greater and the increased risk is therefore tolerable for a short period. They also know that the longer this situation is allowed to persist, the greater the likelihood that it will come to be regarded as normal. They therefore devise rules for themselves to guard against this possibility. In one reported case, managers would draw "a line in the sand" for themselves: if the problem was not fixed by a certain deadline, the plant would be taken out of operation until it was. Hayes, 2009.

often are. As mining operations approached the old workings, water began to seep out of the mine face, indicating that they were dangerously close. However, this indication of danger was dismissed on the grounds that the coal seam was naturally wet and that water seeping out of the mine face was therefore to be expected. In other words, the water was explained away as normal.[12]

The problem is that warning signs may have multiple interpretations, at least one of which is benign. If a benign interpretation can be identified, this can be used to explain away the warning. The anomaly is no longer an anomaly; it is what would be expected in the circumstances; it is normal. This is what happened at the Australian mine. It is also what happened at the Macondo well.

The question then is: how did the Macondo decision-making group normalise or explain away the rise in drill pipe pressure? They did so by invoking a "bladder effect". As described earlier, during the reduced pressure test, the mud in the riser was supported by the rubber seal that had been closed around the drill pipe. This was meant to isolate the water in the cavity below the seal from any downward pressure exerted by the mud. However, according to the bladder theory, the rubber seal was slightly flexible and so it would transmit pressure from the mud above to the water below, which would in turn transmit additional pressure up the drill pipe.[13]

This theory was propounded by the Transocean employees in the group who said that they had seen this phenomenon before when doing tests of this nature and that it was not uncommon. Others in the group had not heard of it, but found themselves persuaded by the logic. Indeed, one of the BP men in the group was still willing to defend the theory a week after the accident.[14] However, according to all of the experts, the bladder effect makes no sense and could not possibly account for the findings. Even if such a mechanism were possible, and some additional pressure had been transmitted up the drill pipe, once the fluid at the top of the pipe had been bled off and the pressure reduced to zero, there is no way the pressure could rise again. The original proponents of the bladder effect died in the accident, so it has not been possible to explore the origins of this theory.

In the cold light of hindsight, the bladder effect has no credibility, but it was sufficiently convincing on the day to serve as an ad hoc explanation for the unexpected pressure readings on the drill pipe. In this way, what should have been an unequivocal warning was normalised.

A faulty mental model

The bladder effect provided the team with an explanation for the high pressures on the drill pipe. This meant that their assumption that the well was secure remained intact. But the team still did not have the evidence they needed to declare the well safe. They began to wonder if they might get the necessary evidence by conducting the test a different way. Accordingly, they decided to conduct the test using a *different line* into the water-filled cavity — the "kill pipe" (see Figure 3.3). This was an unusual but quite defensible way to conduct the test.

First, they filled the kill pipe with water. Next, they opened the valve at the top of the kill pipe, reducing the pressure to zero. Finally, they closed it. This time, the pressure remained at zero, as required. However, the pressure at the top of *drill* pipe remained high. The team debated this difference and ultimately chose to ignore the high drill pipe reading and go with the kill pipe which was registering a steady zero. This was what they were looking for. As BP investigators put it subsequently, the zero pressure on the kill "pipe" was a "powerful stimulus" that seemed to sweep away other doubts. On this basis, they declared that the well had passed the test and that the cement seal was holding.

Unfortunately, their reasoning was utterly confused. The best way to think about this is in terms of mental models and situational awareness. The concept of situational awareness has become a popular way of understanding mistakes made by operators in complex environments — in particular, mistakes made by aircraft pilots.[15] Where such people have wrong or inadequate mental models of the situation they are in, they can make decisions that prove disastrous.

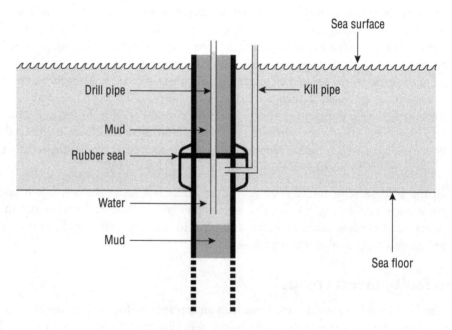

FIGURE 3.3: Test using kill pipe

A relevant example of this is provided by the operators who overfilled the distillation column at the Texas City Refinery, initiating a disastrous explosion. These operators had an erroneous mental model of the situation, believing that that column was nearly empty, when in fact it was nearly full. Their erroneous understanding of the situation stemmed largely from the lack of appropriate instrumentation which would have drawn attention to the level in the column.

Returning to the Macondo team, they were tapping into a water-filled cavity 5,000 ft below, with no possibility of observing directly what was going on. It was vital, therefore, that they have a clear mental picture of what they were doing.

Look again at Figure 3.3 and consider this question: how could the pressure readings at the top of the drill pipe and the kill pipe be different? The two lines, both presumably filled with water, go into the same water-filled cavity or reservoir. If the pressure at the top of either line is reduced to zero, this must automatically reduce the pressure on the other to zero since, if there is any pressure difference, the water will flow from one to the other, via the connecting cavity, in what was known as a U-tube effect, until the pressure is equalised. Given the starting assumptions, that is the way it must be. It is only on that basis that the tests can be regarded as interchangeable.

Yet the equalisation of pressure described above did not happen. The pressure at the top of the drill pipe remained high, while the pressure at the top of the kill pipe was zero. The explanation must be that, for whatever reason, the kill pipe was not in communication with the water-filled cavity below. Subsequent analysis suggests that in fact it was blocked.[16] If the team had had a clear picture of what they were trying to do, they could not have accepted different readings on the two pipes. That difference could only mean that something was wrong with the testing procedure they were using, and that they would need to start all over again.

The question now is: why did the decision-making group, every one of them, lack the requisite mental model? We are back here to questions of competence.

BP officials believed that senior Transocean employees would have had the ability to properly interpret the test,[17] but Transocean itself declared that the people concerned were only "tradesmen" and did not have the necessary training.[18] This difference of opinion has to be understood against the backdrop of legal wrangling about responsibility for the disaster. But the fact is that none of the people involved in the integrity test was a tertiary-trained engineer. The Transocean employees all had very limited formal education and had worked their way up from the drill floor. They had not been trained to think in abstract terms and, arguably, could not be expected to have a clear mental model of how the test should work. As for the BP people, the company man was officially known as a well site leader, but this position had previously been known as drilling foreman. The latter term provides a clue as to the educational level of those who held these positions. Like the Transocean employees, they had limited formal education and their ability to think conceptually would have been correspondingly limited.

All this raises the question of whether tertiary-qualified engineers should have been on site and involved in the decision-making. It was quite startling to many outside observers that none of the drillers on the rig, from the most senior Transocean manager[19] down, had a professional engineering degree. This issue came to prominence following the Longford gas plant accident in Melbourne in 1998, where it was revealed that there were no engineers on site to assist operators on the day of the accident. Had there been, the accident would probably have been avoided.[20]

To this day, companies continue to wrestle with the issue of whether to maintain professional engineers on site, or to locate them at head office and expect site staff to contact them when needed. The view of some BP officials, even after the event, was that well integrity testing was not a sophisticated activity and there was no need to have engineers present; all that was necessary was that decision-makers be provided with a clearer and tighter set of procedures.

The opposite view is taken where corporations aspire to be high reliability organisations, as in sections of the nuclear industry. After the near-meltdown at Three Mile Island in 1979, United States nuclear power stations introduced a position known as a shift technical advisor (STA). This was a person with an engineering degree, trained to the level of senior reactor operator. The STA had no operational duties; rather, the job was to stand back, seek to understand the entire technical system, and help make sense of any anomalies. The nuclear industry found this invaluable in helping to maintain the big picture, that is, in helping to maintain situational awareness.[21]

It is particularly significant that the STA had no regular operational duties. This is an example of the type of redundancy which companies need to be able to tolerate if they aspire to the status of a high reliability organisation. The point has been made as follows in an article entitled "In praise of slack":[22]

> "Organisational slack, in terms of time and human resources that
> are not constantly subject to measures of short-term efficiency,
> is important for organisations coping with the challenges of the
> 21st century …"

To return to the Macondo accident, the regulatory response is based firmly on the idea that decisions such as those taken by the Macondo group need to be taken or at least supervised by experts, in this case, engineers. The regulations now require that there be "certification by a professional engineer that there are two independent, tested barriers" in place.[23]

Groupthink

Up to this point, I have talked about the decision-making process without considering the dynamics of the decision-making group. This must now be addressed. As we shall see, what happened was an example of the well-known process of groupthink.

Consider, first, the composition of the group. For any one shift, there was one BP company man on duty. The decision on the well integrity test was debated and finally taken in a period that covered two shifts,[24] so two company men ended up being involved. The decision-making group thus consisted of two BP company men, accompanied by a trainee, and two long-serving drillers,[25] accompanied by an assistant driller, all of the latter being Transocean employees.[26]

Formally, the decision was the responsibility of the BP company man (or men, in this case). He was authorised by BP to take any decision consistent with BP procedures. If in doubt, or otherwise unable to decide, he was expected to "escalate" the issue to his supervisor, the shore-based well team leader. BP managers believed that their men on the rig should have called them to discuss the problems they were having, and they expressed bewilderment that they had not done so.[27] But BP's own policy discouraged the company man (or men) from calling shore. The policy was to "empower" the company men to take their own decisions,[28] and there is evidence that this policy did affect the judgment made by these two men.[29]

Be that as it may, the real process by which the decision was made departed significantly from the formal situation. According to the Macondo well manager ashore, the reality was that it was a team decision.[30] Furthermore, according to one of the BP investigators, this was as it should be. "All parties need to be comfortable that the test is good", he said.[31] This is a crucial statement. This de facto practice of collective decision-making paved the way for various social psychological processes to take over.

The first is the phenomenon of "risky shift". It has been experimentally demonstrated that groups are often more inclined to make risky decisions than individual group members would make when acting alone.[32] It was argued in an earlier chapter that group decision-making tends to absolve individuals of responsibility, resulting in less than adequate decisions, and there may have been something of that going on here.

However, there was a second and more significant process at work. It is an interesting social psychological fact that, when decisions are to be made by small groups, there is a presumption that they will be unanimous. There is no logical reason why this should be so. In larger groups, we are happy to accept majority decision-making, but in small groups, the presumption is that everyone will agree.

This phenomenon creates difficulties for those who may doubt the wisdom of the dominant view being expressed in the group. Of course, the doubters are in a strong position because they have the power to block consensus. But this in turn means that enormous pressure may be brought to bear on them by other members of the group in order to achieve consensus. This can result in flawed decision-making. The process is known as groupthink

Groupthink is a concept that was first developed by a political scientist to explain certain disastrous US foreign policy decisions made by presidents in consultation with small groups of advisers.[33] It appears that members of these groups who held dissenting views felt unable to speak up. The phenomenon has since been widely studied by experimental social psychologists.[34]

Groupthink has also been used to understand the processes that led to the *Challenger* launch decision. Engineers had warned about the risks of a cold temperature launch. A group of four managers was then called on to make the decision. Three were in favour of launching, while one remained undecided. Eventually, the group leader told him that it was "time to take off his engineering hat and put on his management hat". He capitulated and, as a result, the group leader was able to present the launch recommendation as unanimous.[35]

When applying this perspective to the Macondo decision-making group, it is important to identify where real power lay in the group. Here, we need to understand the culture of the rig. The Transocean rig crew had been together for years and formed a tight-knit group. As any sociologist will tell you, groups of this nature have strong norms, that is, rules about what is and isn't acceptable behaviour. These grow out of the dynamics of the group itself and may have relatively little to do with the rules or procedures of any wider formal organisation of which they are a part. For example, the culture of the school peer group operates within a wider context of school rules but is independent of those rules. The rules of informal groups are enforced by means of informal yet powerful sanctions, one of the most powerful being ridicule.

The culture of the drillers has been described as follows:[36]

> "Drillers are highly skilled technicians who take a personal interest in every well. This small, tightly woven fraternity of opinionated people is very aware of their importance to the success of the project. The majority of skilled drillers are over 50 years old ...
>
> It is a leadership role, by practice if not definition ...
>
> Complexity is reflected in the seemingly unending acronyms, obscure terms freely mixed from any number of professional disciplines, and oilfield slang, add to the complex mind-set. These terms are also a

means to manage the complexity. They form a sort of secret language that binds offshore workers. Complexity is also mitigated by teasing and self-deprecating, competitive humour. Peer pressure is important. No one wants to be branded a 'worm' (slang used to describe someone for asking seemingly 'dumb' questions)."

This was the culture with which the BP company man (or men) had to contend. They were not associated with the rig long term, but came and went. Indeed, on this occasion, one of the two company men had been on the rig for only a few days.

Given all of these circumstances, it was natural for the BP company men to defer to the drillers when they themselves were in doubt. As noted above, the role of the driller is, in practice, a leadership role and clearly the senior driller present exercised leadership in relation to the bladder theory.

The BP company men were at first sceptical of the bladder theory. Then, one of them decided to accept it. That left the other as the sole hold-out against the theory — the one person blocking consensus. This was clearly a difficult situation for him to be in. What made it worse was that, as he told BP interviewers, the "drillers found it humorous" that he was uncomfortable with their explanation of the high pressure on the drill pipe.[37] One can infer from this that they were "teasing" him, to use the language quoted above. This was the culture of the drillers in action — in this case, aimed at bringing not just one of their own into line, but also the BP company man himself.

In the end, the dominant members of the group prevailed. They did not simply silence the doubters, they persuaded them. Such is the power of groupthink. So it was that, as a result of this entirely informal process, the two company men formally declared that the test had been successful.

The report of the Chief Counsel notes that the BP company men failed to exercise "independent judgment regarding the test results … [They] tried to create consensus by accepting the explanation of the rig crew rather than independently verifying the explanation the rig crew had provided".[38] This is much too limited a view. The fact is that the social processes at work made it virtually impossible for them to act independently.

Some solutions

What can be done to ensure that processes like groupthink and normalisation do not operate as they did at the Macondo well?

Obviously, tighter procedures and a more rigorous approach to ensuring competence are necessary. But this chapter has suggested that a fundamental part of the problem was the collective decision-making process. That being so, the solution must be to ensure that one person is responsible for decisions, both in theory *and* in practice.

Collective decision-making is often based on the assumption that the collective wisdom of the group is greater than that of any one member of the group. However, research shows that collective decisions are no better than the decision that would be made by the most expert member of the group.[39] Hence, nothing is lost and much is gained by single-person decision-making, provided that person has the appropriate expertise.

If the decision-maker is to be as effective as possible, this person must be isolated to some extent from the group pressures described above. This does not mean that decision-makers should act in isolation. They of course need to consult, but consultation must be kept conceptually distinct from decision-making. In principle, the decision-maker must in some sense withdraw before making the decision.

The regulatory changes that have been made by the US administration post-Macondo will have this effect. Decisions about whether the cement job is adequate and whether the well is properly sealed will have to be certified by a professional engineer. Such a person will have sole responsibility and will not be able to pass this responsibility to others. Furthermore, such a person will be on site only intermittently and therefore will not be subject to group pressures, as were the BP company men.

In the absence of such regulations, it is important that companies ensure that those who are formally responsible for decisions have the necessary expertise to take those decisions themselves, without having to rely on the informal and uncertain expertise of those around them. We are back here to questions of competence and the need to have professionally qualified people on site to assist with or take important decisions. As noted earlier, the nuclear industry is a model in this respect.

One strategy which is applicable — whether the decision is to be made by a group or an individual — is to appoint a devil's advocate. This involves assigning one person the role of critic, responsible for making the case against whatever may be the proposed course of action. The decision-maker (or makers) needs to consider this case and explicitly reject it before taking action. This would undermine the presumption of consensus that generates groupthink. The devil's advocate role may need to be rotated to ensure that people do not take it personally.*

---

* Klein (2009, pp 234, 235) argues that appointed devil's advocates do not make a positive difference. In the research he quotes, the matter for decision concerns vacation arrangements for company employees. In this situation, devil's advocates were ignored. However, getting it wrong about the best holiday arrangements is not a matter of great consequence, while getting it wrong with respect to catastrophic hazards has enormous consequences. People are likely to be more careful in dismissing the views of an appointed devil's advocate in such circumstances, especially as they will fear being held to account if things go wrong.

There may also be ways to create this position naturally. The safety management plan for an Australian coal mine specified that, when certain incidents occurred — incidents that warned of the possibility of disaster — a decision-making group should be constituted. The plan specified that this group should include an external safety official from the miners' union. This person could be expected to resist group pressures that might lead to the premature dismissal of warnings. On at least one occasion, the strategy proved its worth by preventing the group from making a decision which would have resulted in an underground explosion.[40]

Conclusion

The misinterpretation of the well integrity test has been treated by many observers as a puzzling and inexplicable failure. The one common explanatory thread running through much of the commentary has been that those who carried out the test did not have the necessary competence.

We have seen here, however, that there were various social processes at work that contributed to the outcome: confirmation bias; normalisation of warning signs; inadequate situational awareness; and groupthink. Once these processes are taken into account, the faulty decisions made by the Macondo group become entirely understandable, terrifyingly so. They have contributed to disasters in the past and could easily do so again in other contexts. Organisations operating in hazardous environments need to be alert to these processes and find ways to guard against them.

Endnotes

1   DWI, 25 August, p 156.
2   DWI, 23 August, p 259.
3   Personal communication.
4   Actually, there was spacer fluid between the water and the mud.
5   In fact, a first-reduced pressure test was inconclusive because the rubber around the drill pipe did not seal properly (CCR, p 154).
6   Nickerson, 1998, p 175.
7   Hopkins, 2008, p 44.
8   CCR, p 162.
9   CCR, p 95.
10   Vaughan, 1996.
11   CAIB, 2003.
12   Hopkins, 2000a.
13   CCR, p 157.
14   CCR, p 162.

15 Hudson et al (nd); Salmon et al, 2011; Flin et al, 2008, pp 18, 19.

16 By the spacer.

17 DWI, 26 August, O'Bryan, p 449.

18 CCR, p 240.

19 The OIM (offshore installation manager).

20 Hopkins, 2000.

21 I am indebted to Earl Carnes for this account (personal communication). See also the INPO document "Nuclear power plant shift technical advisor", April 1980, Appendix C to the NRC letter (NUREG-0737), dated November 1980 and titled "Clarification of TMI action plan requirements".

22 Lawson, 2001, p 125. Unfortunately, the STA initiative was not intended to be long term. The long-term goal was to have shift supervisors who were qualified engineers. This would eventually eliminate the element of slack which is praised above, but it would honour the principle that there should be professionally qualified people on site at all times.

23 30 CFR, Pt 250, 14 October 2010, p 63346.

24 DWI, 22 July, pp 234, 235. The decision group spent about three hours conducting the test — a test that would normally take about 45 minutes. DWI, 8 December, am, Robinson, p 81.

25 The more senior of the two was formally a tool pusher.

26 CCR, pp 156, 157.

27 DWI, 7 October, Guide, p 207.

28 DWI, 8 December, am, Robinson, pp 18, 19.

29 CCR, p 336.

30 DWI, 22 July, Guide, p 161.

31 DWI, 8 December, am, Robinson, p 91.

32 Moghadden, 1998, p 465.

33 Janis, 1982.

34 Moghadden, 1998, pp 460–463.

35 Vaughan, 1996, pp 316, 318.

36 P Donley, "This is not about mystics: or why a little science would help a lot", Deepwater Horizon Study Group working paper, January 2011, pp 11, 18.

37 CCR, p 158.

38 CCR, p 240.

39 Hilmer and Donaldson, 1996, pp 69, 70; Yetton and Bottger, 1982, pp 307–321.

40 Hopkins, 2002.

CHAPTER 4

FALLING DOMINOS: THE FAILURE OF DEFENCE-IN-DEPTH

A series of defences or controls should have prevented the Macondo blowout. If even one of those defences had worked as intended, the accident would not have happened. But *all* of them failed. How could that be? Was this pure coincidence or was there something systematic about these failures? This chapter provides an answer.

Let us think abstractly for a moment. Accidents in well-defended systems occur only when all of the defences fail simultaneously. Using the Swiss cheese metaphor, they occur only when the holes all line up. Assuming that the holes are independent of each other, the probability that they will all line up, that is, that all the barriers will fail simultaneously, should be infinitesimally small. From this point of view, a major accident is a freak event, against all odds.

But there is another possibility: that the barrier failures are not independent events. Instead, the barriers are connected in ways that make multiple failures more likely. This is what happened in the Macondo accident. The use of multiple barriers to protect against a catastrophic event is known as "defence-in-depth". The argument here, then, is that it was the whole strategy of defence-in-depth that failed. Moreover, as we shall see, the reasons it failed are likely to operate in many other situations where reliance is placed on this strategy.

This chapter is divided into two parts. Part 1 looks at some of the barrier failures that allowed the blowout to take place. Part 2 looks at failures *after* the blowout, as a result of which the blowout developed into both a human and an environmental catastrophe.

Part 1: Pre-blowout barrier failures

For present purposes, I want to concentrate on the following four failures and to demonstrate how they interacted:

(1) the failure of the cement job,

    — coupled with the declaration of success, and

    — the decision not to use a cement evaluation tool;

(2) the failure of the well integrity test;

(3) the failure of monitoring; and

(4) the failure of the blowout preventer (BOP).

This sequence is summarised in Figure 4.1 for ready reference. I shall deal with the first two quite briefly since they have been discussed in detail in earlier chapters.

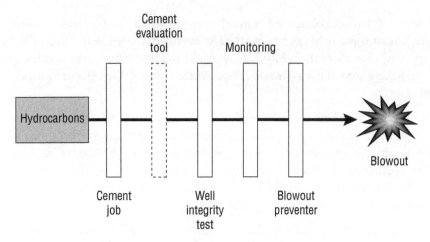

FIGURE 4.1: Pre-blowout barrier failures

The cement job

A good cement job at the bottom of the well is vital for blowout prevention. It is a physical barrier that is supposed to be put in place when drilling has been completed and the rig is about to move on to its next assignment.

Despite the importance of this physical barrier, the cement job was not designed in a way that maximised its chances of success. As we saw, a number of design decisions were taken that were widely seen at the time as increasing the risk of failure. I shall show here that this was judged to be acceptable on the assumption that subsequent defences would work as intended.

As was noted in Chapter 2, a Macondo engineer wrote about one of the risky cementing decisions as follows: "But who cares, it's done, end of story, [we] will *probably* be fine" (emphasis added). This comment implicitly recognises that, in order to be certain, the team would need to rely on subsequent evaluation and testing, such as the well integrity test.

A further instance of this attitude was described in Chapter 2. Prior to pumping cement into the well, a valve at the bottom of the well needed to be activated. This required drilling fluid pressure to be increased. To the surprise and concern of everyone, it took *six times* the expected pressure to make something happen and, even then, no one was quite sure *what* had happened. (Had something broken?) Matters became even more mysterious when it subsequently took *less* pressure than expected to keep drilling fluid moving. These were anomalous events that cast doubt over whether the cement job would be effective. However, the team decided to ignore them and rely on later integrity testing to establish whether or not these events had prevented the cement from sealing the well.[1] Unfortunately, the importance being placed on the later test was never communicated to those who carried it out.

The use of nitrified or foam cement was another factor that increased the risk that the cement job might fail. The senior Transocean man on the rig expressed doubts about the nitrified cement and commented at the time: "I guess that is what we have those pinchers for." This was a reference to the BOP sitting on the sea floor on top of the well. The BOP was equipped with powerful sheers that, in theory, could cut through the drill pipe and close off the well completely, if the worst came to the worst. These were the pinchers that the Transocean manager was referring to which, in his mind, compensated for the increased risk of using nitrified cement.[2] The senior BP man on the rig evidently had the same concern. He was heard to say "be careful with the nitrogen and be ready to close the bag", another reference to the BOP.[3] In other words, both of these men were doubtful about the cement job but assumed that the last line of defence, the BOP, would save the day if necessary. We shall examine shortly why that faith was misplaced.

We see, then, that there was quite widespread recognition that the circumstances of the cement job increased the risk of failure and that many people in their own minds were relying on *subsequent* defences to function properly should the cement job in fact fail.

The declaration of success

Once the team had finished pumping the cement, a subtle change in thinking occurred. They knew that the cement had got to its intended location, because they had had full returns. On this basis, they announced that the cement job had been successful, even before the cement had set. In so doing, they took no account of the other ways in which the cement might have failed (eg by nitrogen breakout or by contamination with mud). Previous reservations seemed to disappear and the cement job was implicitly assumed to be a success in every respect.

The decision not to use the cement evaluation tool

One consequence of the declaration of success was the decision not to evaluate the quality of the cement using a cement bond log, as discussed in Chapter 2. The use of this tool would probably have revealed the failure of the cement job. However, I shall not treat it here as a separate barrier failure because it was never intended to be an independent barrier. The intention was to use a cement bond log only if there were other indications that the cement job might have failed. For this reason, in barrier diagrams in this book, it is represented with a dotted line.

The well integrity test

The well integrity test was a pivotal point in the strategy of defence-in-depth. This was the test that would establish definitively whether the cement had sealed the well. This was the test that the engineers had relied on, when they thought about it, to resolve whatever uncertainties they may have had about the success of the cement job.

But the engineers were not directly involved in carrying out the test. That was the job of the BP man on the rig, together with the Transocean drillers. These people did not see the test as pivotal. The cement job had already been declared a success and, from their point of view, the well integrity test was just a routine activity designed to confirm what they already knew. As we saw in Chapter 3, these men were profoundly affected by a confirmation bias that prevented them from even contemplating that the well might not be sealed. The Chief Counsel's report puts it nicely:[4]

> "[The testers] began with the assumption that the cement job had been successful and kept running tests and proposing explanations until they convinced themselves that their assumption was correct."

The point is that this was no longer an independent line of defence. It was entirely undermined by beliefs about earlier lines of defence. It failed precisely because of the earlier mistaken announcement that the cement job had been a success.

The failure of monitoring

The next failure in the sequence was the failure of monitoring. For nearly an hour before mud and gas began to spill uncontrollably onto the rig floor, there were clear indications of what was about to happen. Had people been monitoring the well, as they were supposed to, they would have recognised these indications and taken preventive action. So why were they not monitoring the well?

To answer this question, we need some more background information. Drilling operations involve a constant circulation of fluids into and out of the well. Normally these flows are in balance. But if oil and gas are entering the bottom of the well, then outflow will exceed inflow and the well is said to be "flowing". It is fundamental to the safe operation of a drilling rig that flows in and out of a well be continuously monitored so that excess flows can be detected rapidly and the well shut in, long before the escaping oil and gas reach the surface.

Normally, fluids going into the well are drawn from an input tank or "pit", while fluids coming out of the well go into an outflow pit. There are instruments that measure the levels in these pits. The volume in the pit receiving fluid from the well should increase at the same rate as the volume in the pit delivering fluid to the well decreases. If it increases at a faster rate, the well is likely to be flowing. There is even an alarm that can be set to indicate when volume changes in one pit are significantly different from volume changes in the other. This comparison of volume *in* with volume *out* is the most basic and also the most reliable indicator of whether a well is flowing.

There were two groups of people on the *Deepwater Horizon* with responsibility for monitoring flows. First, there were the drillers and their assistants, all employees of the rig owner, Transocean. Second, BP had employed another organisation, Sperry Sun,[5] to provide an independent monitoring service. A Sperry Sun employee, known as a mudlogger, was on duty at all times on the rig.

On the afternoon of the accident, the heavy mud in the riser was being replaced with lighter seawater, so that the riser could be removed, prior to the rig's departure. At some point in this operation, the well would become underbalanced, meaning that the weight of mud in the well and riser would no longer be enough to counterbalance the pressure of oil and gas in the reservoir. At that stage, the well would begin to flow, unless there was at least one effective cement barrier in place. But the cement job had failed, so the well indeed began to flow from the moment the well became underbalanced.

However, for several hours that afternoon, the Transocean rig crew had made it impossible to reliably monitor flows coming out of the well. Instead of running the outflow into a tank where the volume could be measured, they were offloading it directly to a supply vessel alongside the rig, in order to save time. The mudlogger pointed out to the Transocean crew that this prevented her from doing her monitoring job properly, but her complaint went unheeded.[6] Later, for reasons that need not be discussed here, the crew began running the outflow fluid directly overboard into the sea, again making it impossible to monitor volume changes accurately. This second period of discharge occurred at the very time that the well was flowing and masked the indications that would otherwise have been apparent to the mudlogger (a second mudlogger was now on duty, there having been a shift change in the interim).[7]

It is clear from this account that the drilling crew took actions that prevented the mudloggers from doing their job effectively. The capacity of the drillers themselves to monitor the well was similarly affected.

Despite the reservations of the mudloggers,[8] bypassing the outflow pit in this way may well have been the norm. As one Transocean employee said: "... pumping to the boat was just something the rig did."[9] Moreover, these operations were happening at the same time as a group of senior executives from both BP and Transocean were visiting the rig. Interestingly, they did not question what was happening, suggesting that they saw nothing abnormal about the practice. Even if this inference is disputed, what is clear is that the personnel on the rig that afternoon had no sense that what they were doing might be in any way questionable or that they should desist while ever these senior executives were on board.

So why were the drillers behaving in this way, with so little concern about whether the monitoring was being done effectively? What was their state of mind?

As far as they were concerned, the job was over. According to one inquiry witness: "... when you get to that point, everyone goes to the mindset that we're through; this job is done."[10] The well had been drilled and it had twice been declared safe, once when the engineers announced that the cement job had been successful, and again when the BP man on the rig declared that the well had passed the integrity test. The crew was now just finishing up and, from their point of view, it was unnecessary to monitor the well closely. Moreover, they were in a hurry. Tank cleaners were coming on board at midnight and the mud needed to be moved before they could start work.[11] If the short cuts they were taking interfered with the capacity of the mudloggers to do their job, so be it.

The result of this mindset was that another of the defences to blowout was completely defeated. It was presumed to be unnecessary precisely because of the operation of earlier defences.

The blowout preventer

In deepwater drilling, the blowout preventer (BOP) sits on the sea floor on top of the well. The drill pipe passes through it on its way from the rig to the well bottom. The BOP has two main modes of operation. First, it can be used to close a well during normal operations, as is required from time to time. Second, in an emergency, it can be used to sheer through the drill pipe and seal the well.

In this emergency mode, the BOP was regarded by many as a last line of defence. If all else failed, the BOP would save them. This was an explicit assumption of various people involved in the drilling of the Macondo well. But this faith was misplaced for the following reasons.

First, there is the record of failure. In 2009, Transocean commissioned a confidential study of the reliability of BOPs used by deepwater rigs. According to the *New York Times*,[12] the study:

> "… found 11 cases where crews on deepwater rigs had lost control of their wells and then activated blowout preventers to prevent a spill. In only six of those cases were the wells brought under control, leading the researchers to conclude that in actual practice, blowout preventers used by deepwater rigs had a 'failure' rate of 45 per cent."

These are shocking findings. They indicate that no one should ever have relied on the BOP to operate effectively in an emergency. This was a defence that provided an entirely false sense of security.

More fundamentally, there were design limitations of the BOP in use on the *Deepwater Horizon*. The pipe used to drill a well consists of sections that screw together. The metal thickness at these joints is double the normal drill pipe thickness. The joints amount to 10% of pipe length. It was known that the BOP could not sheer through these joints. From this point of view, if the BOP is called on to sheer through the pipe to close off the well in an emergency, there is a 10% chance that it will fail. This fact in itself should have cautioned against reliance on the BOP as the ultimate saviour.

Furthermore, the BOP was not designed to deal with a blowout that was already at full throttle.[13] The design assumption was that the crew would be monitoring the well at all times and that they would quickly recognise when they had lost control of the well. They would therefore activate the BOP long before the material began spewing out on the deck of the rig. At the Macondo well, the blowout developed unrecognised and unchecked, causing the drill pipe inside the BOP to buckle and bend.[14] As a result, when the BOP sheers were activated, they were unable to sheer through the pipe.[15]

Interestingly, a Transocean risk assessment carried out in 2000 identified the failure by operators to act *quickly* as a major threat to the reliability of the BOP.[16] Here, then, is the nub of the matter. The BOP did not operate independently of previous barriers. It depended for its effectiveness on the alertness of the drillers on the rig. Given that they had dropped their guard, the BOP was quite unreliable as a barrier against blowout.

There is a paradox here. If a well is being monitored properly, drillers will shut it in long before they lose control and there will be no need for the BOP to operate in emergency mode. On the other hand, if a blowout occurs because the well is not being monitored, these are the very circumstances in which the BOP is least likely to operate effectively. In short, the emergency function of the BOP offers little protection beyond that offered by the monitoring activity of an alert crew. Had this been understood by those concerned, they would have placed far less trust in their BOP.

A summary

The barriers under discussion can now be seen to be intimately connected. The engineers took risky decisions about cementing on the assumption that the well integrity test would identify any problems. Some of the Macondo team looked further along the line of defences to the BOP, which they saw as the ultimate defence should the cement job fail. Prior to the cement job then, people were looking to *subsequent* barriers to make up for any deficiencies. Then came the declaration that the cement job had been a success, based on full returns. Accordingly, the cement evaluation tool was dispensed with. Moreover, the people responsible for subsequent defences now began to look *back* to earlier defences as their guarantee of safety. The well integrity test results were misinterpreted because the engineers had declared the cement job a success, and well monitoring was effectively abandoned because of the two earlier declarations of success. Finally, the BOP failed in large part because the monitoring had failed. Once the engineers mistakenly declared the cement job a success, subsequent barriers were all effectively nullified. A more extraordinary failure of the whole philosophy of defence-in-depth is hard to imagine.

The other important aspect of this account is that it reveals that there was no real commitment to the philosophy of defence-in-depth. No one really believed in the importance of multiple barriers. One good barrier was enough. There are some deep-seated reasons for this type of thinking that I shall deal with in Chapter 8.

Before moving on, it needs to be said that the belief that one barrier is enough is by no means a universal way of thinking in hazardous industries. Hayes has studied decision-making by senior site managers in organisations that approach the high reliability organisation ideal.[17] She found them committed to the principles of defence-in-depth. If they discovered that not all of the barriers were in place, they took the view that the system was not safe and something had to be done. Hayes found that they adopted one of two options:

(1) stop/limit/curtail production to within the limits of the remaining barriers; or

(2) provide a temporary replacement barrier (which might simply be increased monitoring by the operational team).

Such thinking was not in evidence on the *Deepwater Horizon*.

Part 2: Post-blowout barrier failures

There were two largely independent consequences of the Macondo blowout. The first was an explosion, with major loss of life. The second was the oil spill, with catastrophic environmental consequences. This makes the Macondo blowout unusual. Some of the best-known blowouts, such as the Santa Barbara blowout off the coast of California in 1969 and the Montarra blowout off the coast of Western Australia in 2009, resulted in major oil spills, but there was no ignition[18] and no loss of life.

The fact that the Macondo blowout had two independent disastrous consequences means, in effect, that two independent sets of post-blowout barriers failed. The Swiss cheese model presumes a linear sequence of barriers and cannot be used to represent this situation. We need to generalise the model in some way. The bow tie model of accident causation and prevention does just that (see Figure 4.2).[19] A bow tie model identifies a major accident event, such as a blowout, labeled here as a "top event".* It allows for the possibility of more than one pathway to this event, and more than one pathway leading from the event. Barriers must be established on each of these pathways to prevent the major accident event or ameliorate its consequences.

In the case of the Macondo blowout, we are interested in two pathways from the event, one leading to the explosion and loss of life, and the other to the catastrophic oil spill. We shall focus on two potential barriers on each of these pathways (see Figure 4.3).

In relation to the upper path in the diagram, if the gas from the blowout had been diverted overboard, the risk of explosion would have been considerably less. Similarly, if the rig had been designed to prevent gas from reaching all potential ignition sources, the explosion might have been averted. In relation to the lower path, if BP had had an effective blowout response plan or, failing that, an effective oil spill response plan, the environmental damage might have been much reduced.

The argument in Part 2 of this chapter is that BP consistently downplayed the importance of post-blowout barriers, either by placing reliance on pre-blowout

---

* This terminology makes no sense in the bow tie context. It comes from fault tree analysis, where it does make sense.

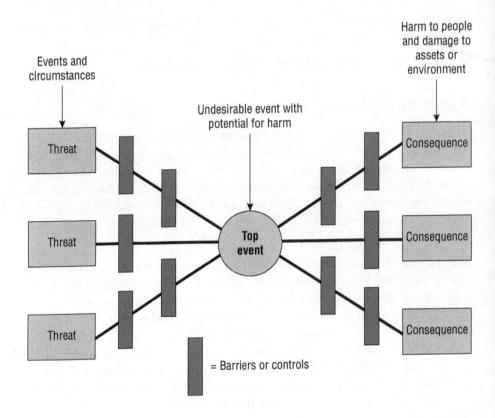

Events and
circumstances

Harm to people
and damage to
assets or
environment

Undesirable event with
potential for harm

Threat

Threat

Threat

Top
event

Consequence

Consequence

Consequence

= Barriers or controls

FIGURE 4.2: Simple bow tie diagram

barriers or by underestimating in some other way the significance of post-blowout consequences.

The diverter

The rig was equipped with a diverter that allowed mud and gas to be diverted overboard, either to port or starboard. If the winds were favourable, this would carry the gas away from the vessel. Even with unfavourable winds, diversion overboard would reduce the chance of explosion. A study by the regulator revealed that, in 16 out of 20 times that blowouts had been diverted overboard, an explosion had been averted.[20]

One consequence of diversion overboard is that the oil-based drilling fluid (mud) would end up in the sea, constituting a spill, a reportable environmental event.

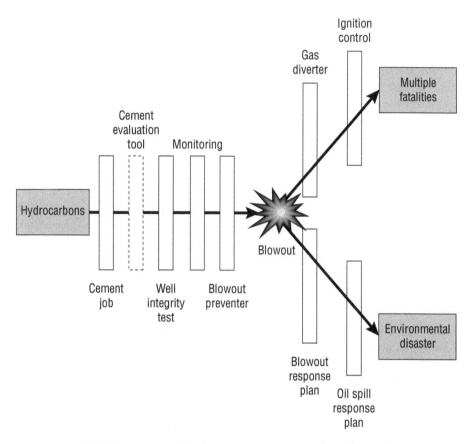

FIGURE 4.3: Simplified bow tie for the Macondo blowout

There was, therefore, another option associated with the diverter. The crew could close a valve and route the flow through a device that separated the gas from the mud. This device vented the gas away from the rig floor and allowed the mud to be retained on board, thereby avoiding a spill. This was an appropriate strategy when the flow was relatively small. But the mud/gas separator could not cope with large flows. Using it in such circumstances would inevitably generate a gas cloud on the rig floor.

When the Macondo blowout began, the crew activated the diverter, but instead of sending the flow overboard, they sent it through the mud/gas separator which was quickly overwhelmed, generating a gas cloud on the rig. It is easy to say in retrospect that this was a serious error of judgment. The question then is: why did they make this mistake?

Transocean's position was that the crew was simply following standard procedures,[21] according to which diversion overboard was a last resort. The procedures, in other words, undermined the effectiveness of the diverter as a barrier against explosion. Furthermore, the diverter had earlier been *set* to divert the flow through the mud/gas separator, not overboard, and it required an active intervention by the crew to switch it to the overboard position.[22] If the primary consideration had been to make this barrier as effective as possible, the default valve setting would have been overboard. The fact that is wasn't meant that the primary consideration was avoiding small-scale environmentally reportable spills.[23] Putting this another way, the crew was more attuned to low-consequence high-probability events, like spills, than it was to high-consequence low-probability events, such as explosions. This is a theme we shall take up in Chapter five. But the important point in the present context is this: since so little thought was given to maximising the effectiveness of the diverter as a barrier against explosion, all concerned must simply have assumed that earlier barriers would perform as intended.

Ignition control

Rig design takes account of the potential for an explosive air/gas mixture to be present at various locations. The design of the *Deepwater Horizon* envisaged small amounts of gas produced by drilling operations accumulating in the drilling areas of the rig. This was therefore defined as a hazardous area, and electrical equipment within this area was designed to be explosion-proof.[24]

However, the engine room was not designated a hazardous area and was not designed to make it impossible for gas to come in contact with ignition sources.[25] On the night in question, the cloud of gas migrated into an engine room and was most likely ignited by an engine.[26] One of the official reports subsequently identified this failure to treat the engine room as a hazardous area as a "risk enhancer",[27] while another called it a "possible contributing cause to the explosion".[28]

One is entitled to ask: on what basis was the engine room designated a non-hazardous area? The answer is that an explosive air/gas mixture was not expected to be present in the engine room.[29] In other words, the classification implicitly discounted the possibility of an event such as the Macondo blowout. The only basis for discounting this possibility is the assumption that earlier defences will have worked to prevent such a blowout from occurring.

Despite the non-hazardous classification, the possibility that gas might enter an engine room had in fact been foreseen, and rig personnel were supposed to manually close the air intakes into the engine room in this event.[30] Perhaps not surprisingly, given the chaotic situation they faced, the crew of the *Deepwater Horizon* did not do so. BP's own comment on this situation is that:[31]

"… there was a high level of reliance upon manual/human intervention in the activation of the *Deepwater Horizon* safety systems … The reliability of the systems was therefore limited by the capability of individuals to respond in a stressed environment."

The regulator went one step further in its official report:[32]

"Absence of emergency shutdown devices that could be *automatically* triggered in response to high gas levels on the rig was a possible contributing cause of the *Deepwater Horizon* explosion." (emphasis added)

According to a United Kingdom analyst, this aspect of the design of the *Deepwater Horizon* would not have been acceptable under the UK safety case regulatory regime.[33] At the very least, air intakes to the engine room would have been equipped with automatic trip mechanisms that would have activated automatically on the detection of gas.[34] This, he said, had been one of the lessons from the Piper Alpha disaster in 1988. He goes on:[35]

"… it would appear that almost a quarter of a century after 167 people were killed because gas entered a Non Hazardous Area containing sources of ignition this apparently happened again on the *Deepwater Horizon*."

The lack of a blowout response plan

Consider now the other consequence stemming from the blowout, the catastrophic oil spill. Logically, there are two things that need to be done to avoid an environmental disaster. The blowout must be stopped, and whatever has been released must be cleaned up. In relation to the former, BP had no plan to deal with oil and gas flowing uncontrollably from the sea floor a mile below the sea surface, other than drilling a relief well to intersect the blowout well and pumping the blowout well full of cement.[36] This would leave the blowout well flowing uncontrollably for many weeks until the relief well could be drilled. Of course, when it came to the point, BP improvised brilliantly and, since that time, great progress has been made in cap-and-contain technology that can be used to stem such a flow. But at the time, BP executives admitted that they were making it up day-to-day and that they did not have "proven equipment and technology" to deal with a blowout.

The exploration plan filed with the regulator before BP began drilling the Macondo well contained the following statements:[37]

"Deepwater well control

BP Exploration and Production Inc, MMS company number 02481, has the financial capability to drill a relief well and conduct other emergency well control operations.

Blowout scenario

A scenario for a potential blowout of the well from which BP would expect to have the highest volume of liquid hydrocarbons is not required for the operations proposed in this EP [exploration plan]."

These statements demonstrate a minimalist, box-ticking approach to the regulatory requirements for the exploration plan. There is no evidence anywhere in the plan that BP had considered how it would deal with a blowout. Again, we are left with the impression that BP assumed either that the earlier defences would work to prevent a blowout or that, if one occurred, the oil spill response plan would work as intended to prevent serious environmental harm. In other words, the assumption that other defences would work as intended relieved them of any need to think carefully about how they would stem a deepwater blowout.[38]

The oil spill response plan

Although the regulator did not require a *blowout* response plan, it did require an *oil spill* response plan and an environmental impact assessment (EIA). These documents seriously underestimated the possible environmental consequences. According to the EIA:[39]

"An accidental oil spill from the proposed activities could cause impacts to beaches. However, due to the distance from the shore (48 miles) and the response capabilities that would be implemented, no significant impacts are expected."

The exploration plan also contains the following passage, which turns out to have been wildly optimistic:

"In the event of an unanticipated blowout resulting in an oil spill, it is unlikely to have an impact based on the industry wide standards for using proven equipment and technology for such responses, implementation of BP's Regional Oil Spill Response Plan which address available equipment and personnel, techniques for containment and recovery and removal of the oil spill."

In some respects, the oil spill response plan and the EIA were examples of what one writer has called "fantasy documents" — documents that companies produce to demonstrate to regulators and the public how they would deal with catastrophic events.[40] Perhaps the clearest evidence of the fantasy nature of these documents is the mention in the oil spill response plan of the need to protect sea lions, sea otters and walruses, none of which exist in the Gulf of Mexico.[41] It is clear that, although BP had prepared various documents to satisfy regulatory requirements, there were no effective post-blowout barriers against environmental disaster.

Explaining the absence of effective post-blowout barriers

A major reason for the lack of attention to post-blowout barriers was BP's reliance on pre-blowout controls. This is very clear in a generic risk assessment that BP did in 2009 for loss-of-well-control in the Gulf of Mexico. That assessment identifies fire and explosion, as well as environmental damage, as possible consequences of a blowout, but the mitigation strategies that it envisages are all focused on preventing a blowout in the first place, not on limiting its consequences once it has occurred. Chief among these strategies is well control training. There is no mention of a blowout response plan or an oil spill response plan.

There is a dilemma here. The best way to deal with blowouts is to prevent them from occurring at all. Prevention is always preferable to emergency response. But a complete strategy for managing major hazards must include measures to mitigate the effect of a major accident event once it has occurred.[42] From this point of view, it was not enough for BP to rely on pre-blowout barriers. It would clearly have been desirable for BP to insist on better explosion prevention systems on the rigs that it contracted to do its drilling, and to have developed a cap-and-contain system to bring blowout wells under control.

It would seem that BP implemented post-blowout controls only to the extent required by regulations. So, given that the fire protection systems required in the Gulf of Mexico were less stringent than those in UK waters, the standards of fire protection on rigs used by BP in the Gulf of Mexico were lower than in the UK.[43] Likewise, BP's attention to blowout and oil spill response was limited to what was required by the regulator. And given that the regulator did not have the resources to effectively scrutinise and challenge exploration plans provided to it, when it came to the crunch, those plans had very little substance. There could be no greater demonstration of the importance of effective regulation. This is a matter that I shall return to in Chapter 10.

If we focus for a moment on safety as opposed to environmental risk, there is another factor that helps to account for the apparent lack of concern about the effectiveness of post-blowout barriers. The generic Gulf of Mexico risk assessment formally assessed the safety risk posed by a blowout as "low". This is a somewhat surprising assessment. In fact, it was explicitly based on the belief that a loss-of-well-control event would be preceded by flow/pressure indicators that would allow time for the safe evacuation of personnel. The presumption here is that the crew would be monitoring these indicators effectively. In other words, the assessment of the risk as "low" depends on the assumption that an earlier defence has worked. Obviously, on that assumption, there is little point in worrying about subsequent defences. From this point of view, reliance on an earlier defence can be seen to have undermined any commitment to ensure the effectiveness of post-blowout defences.

The assessment that the safety risk was "low" had a further consequence. BP's policy was that a low-level risk could be approved by a low-level manager. So it was that, from a safety point of view, the mitigations to deal with the risk of a catastrophic blowout needed the approval of the well team leader only. The problem is that some of the more effective risk management strategies are way beyond the control of such a low-level manager. Consider, for example: improving the design of BOPs so that they function more reliably in extreme circumstances; changing rig designs so that they are less vulnerable to explosion; automating monitoring systems; and implementing more rigorous engineering standards. All of these strategies require resourcing commitments that can only be made at the highest corporate level. BP's designation of the safety risk as low militated against any such high-level involvement. Risk assessments of this nature are notoriously unreliable, in the sense that independent assessors frequently come to quite different judgments about the level of risk.[44] It is therefore disturbing to find companies concluding that a catastrophic blowout may not be a risk that requires close scrutiny at the highest level.

An aside on risk assessment

The uncertainties of the risk assessment process can be further illustrated in the present case. As distinct from the *generic* blowout risk assessment discussed above, the Macondo team carried out a *Macondo-specific* risk assessment prior to the drilling of the well. As was shown in Chapter 2, this risk assessment focused on commercial risk only, even though it was supposed to cover safety risk as well. It is instructive to go back and apply this risk assessment tool to the safety risk of a Macondo-style blowout. The tool requires us to assess *impact* level and *probability*, and then to combine these into a single assessment of risk (see Appendix 2). A Macondo-style blowout, resulting in one or more fatalities, would be classified as "very high" *impact*. As for *probability*, the categories range from very low to high.

"Very low" is defined as: "it could only occur as the result of multiple, independent system or control failures. Future occurrence thought most unlikely. No comparable occurrence is known."

"Low" is defined as: "it could result from a plausible combination of system or control failures. Would probably occur if the system were to be operated for long enough. Comparable events are known to have occurred in the past."

Let us give BP the benefit of the doubt and rate the probability of a Macondo-style incident as "very low", on the basis that "no comparable occurrence is known". The assessment tool next requires that the risk be assessed on a five-point scale: very low, low, moderate, high, very high. A "very high" impact event that has a "very low" probability is classified as a "moderate" risk. In short, the risk of a Macondo-style incident lies at the mid-point of the five-point risk scale. This is not a conclusion that BP drew because it did not ever apply its risk assessment tool in this way. One wonders, if it had, whether it would have devoted more resources to dealing with the safety risks of a blowout.

Notice that the definition of "very low" probability includes the stipulation that the barrier failures are independent. We now know that they were not independent at the Macondo blowout. If we allow for the possibility that barriers may not be independent, we would need to rate the probability of a Macondo-style event as low, rather than very low. The risk level would then change to "high". This would be unacceptable on almost any view.

The discrepancy between the generic blowout safety risk assessment (low) and the Macondo-specific version (moderate or high) highlights the uncertainties of the risk assessment process and the importance of considering the assumptions on which they are based. Because catastrophic incidents are rare, risk assessments of them are not likely to be called into question in the normal course of events. Their assumptions and biases therefore lie undisturbed until an incident like the Macondo blowout causes the spotlight to be shone on them. If companies cannot be relied on to assess realistically the risk of rare but catastrophic events, it is important that regulators do their utmost to check the reasoning of risk assessments that are submitted to them. The regulator in the Gulf of Mexico at the time was not resourced to do this.

Beyond-design-basis events

The Macondo Presidential Commission encouraged the oil and gas sector to look to the nuclear industry for strategies for handling major accident risk. As it happens, a recent development in the nuclear industry has considerable relevance to this discussion. Following the Fukushima nuclear power plant accident in Japan in 2011, the US Nuclear Regulatory Commission set up a task force to identify lessons for the US nuclear industry.[45] The task force noted that the tsunami that triggered the accident was far more severe than the plant had been designed to withstand. It therefore advocated that the Commission's traditional philosophy of defence-in-depth be strengthened by including a requirement to take account of beyond-design-basis events, such as major earthquakes, aircraft impact, and so-called "beyond-design-basis fires and explosions". This is a challenging idea that could well be implemented in the oil and gas industry. It encourages risk assessors to imagine events which are beyond the capacity of their systems to deal with, and to consider what might be the appropriate way of responding to such events.* There is a paradox here in that, as you begin to design for such an event, it is no longer a beyond-design-basis event. It is a creative paradox, however, in that it amounts to a strategy of continuous risk reduction. The significance of this approach is that it explicitly invites attention to situations in which all of the defences have failed. This prevents analysts from implicitly relying on earlier defences, as seems to have happened with BP's post-blowout scenario planning. It is one that all hazardous industries might contemplate.

Conclusion

The strategy of defence-in-depth should mean that the probability of a major accident is vanishingly small. That is clearly not the case. One explanation is that the barriers are not independent of each other. That is what happened at Macondo. Post-blowout barriers were entirely inadequate, in part because safety system designers were relying on pre-blowout barriers to do their job. As for the pre-blowout barriers, the presumption that one had operated successfully seemed to nullify all of the others. Once the engineers mistakenly announced that the cement job had been successful, all of the other barriers collapsed, like falling dominos. Defence-in-depth can only work if the barriers operate independently of each other. That surely is one of the most significant lessons of the Macondo disaster.

---

* The Fukushima power station was designed to handle the worst tsunami that had occurred in the area in the previous 1,000 years; it was not designed to handle the worst possible tsunami, or even the worst tsunami that had occurred in other parts of the world. See C Perrow, "Fukushima and the inevitability of accidents", at http://bos.sagepub.com/content/67/6/44. Had the power station been designed on the latter basis, the Fukushima accident would not have happened. See also *New York Times*, 27 March 2011. Nancy Leveson writes persuasively about the need to take seriously the worst *conceivable* scenario, not just the worst *likely* scenario (Leveson, 2011.)

Endnotes

1. CCR, p 90.
2. DWI, 26 May, p 132; DWI, 27 May, pp 57, 106.
3. DWI, 27 May, Harrell, p 72.
4. CCR, p 161.
5. A subsidiary of Halliburton.
6. BP, 2010, p 91.
7. During the critical period when the well was flowing, the drillers were also engaged in other activities (emptying trip tanks) that made it impossible for the mudlogger to do his job properly.
8. DWI, 7 December, Keith, p 94.
9. DWI, 9 July, Bertone, p 350.
10. BOEMRE, p 86.
11. DWI, 8 December, pm, Spraghe, p 50.
12. 20 June 2010.
13. See the discussion in Transocean, 2011, sec 3.4.5, 3.4.6, 3.4.7. See also BOEMRE, p 145; and National Academy of Engineers report, ch 3.
14. The conditions that led to buckling were present from the moment the well began flowing (BOEMRE, p 140), and meant that the buckling "likely occurred at or near the time when control of the well was lost" (BOEMRE, p 5).
15. According to BOEMRE (p 151), the much-discussed maintenance deficiencies played no role in the failure of the BOP to close properly, nor did various leaks in the BOP (BOEMRE, p 153).
16. See http://documents.nytimes.com/documents-on-the-oil-spill#document/p40.
17. Hayes, 2012.
18. At least, not at the time. The rig involved in the Montarra spill did catch fire many days after the event.
19. Bice and Hayes, 2009.
20. CCR, p 200.
21. CCR, p 201.
22. CCR, p 196.
23. CCR, p 196.
24. Transocean, 2011, sec 3.5.3.
25. Transocean, 2011, p 190.
26. Transocean, 2011, p 190. BOEMRE (p 15) states that, apart from the engines, the mud/gas separator was another possible source of ignition.
27. US Coast Guard, *Deepwater Horizon investigation report*, p M-3.
28. BOEMRE, p 126.
29. B Campbell, "Analysis of cause of explosion on *Deepwater Horizon*", 24 June 2010, paper posted on the Deepwater Horizon Study Group website, 5 August 2010, p 7.
30. BP, 2010, pp 132, 139.
31. BP, 2010, p 139.
32. BOEMRE, p 198.

33   Campbell, op cit.

34   Campbell, op cit, p 7.

35   Campbell, op cit, p 8. Both the Transocean report and the BOEMRE report explain the absence of automatic trips on the basis that the rig was dynamically positioned and needed to be able to use its engines in the event of an emergency (Transocean, p 190; BOEMRE, p 116). The argument is hard to follow. If the situation requires that the air intake be shut off, it is surely better to do this automatically rather than rely on a human who will be predictably unreliable.

36   OSC, p 273.

37   The normal requirement for a blowout scenario is specified at 30 CFR 250.213(g).

38   After the Macondo accident, the regulator imposed a requirement that operators demonstrate that they have the capacity to cap and contain a blowout on the sea floor. See NTL 2010 N10. The oil majors have created a marine well containment company to provide this service.

39   See www.gomr.boemre.gov/PI/PDFImages/PLANS/29/29977.pdf, sec 7.1 and 14.2.2.

40   Clarke, 1999.

41   OSC, p 84.

42   For instance, the provision of blast-proof accommodation for personnel, and automatic firefighting systems.

43   See the article by B Campbell cited earlier.

44   Pickering and Cowley, 2011.

45   The near-term task force review of insights from the Fukushima Dai-Ichi accident, Recommendations for enhancing reactor safety in the 21st century, 12 July 2011, US Nuclear Regulatory Commission.

CHAPTER 5

THE MEANING OF SAFETY

Having identified the sequence of barrier failures that led to the Macondo disaster, we can begin to examine in more detail some of the organisational reasons that gave rise to these failures. Consider the Macondo engineers and their flawed decision-making. The most striking thing about these engineers was the way that they had lost sight of safety risk. Safety was just not on their agenda. This chapter helps us understand why.

One of the lessons that emerged from the BP Texas City Refinery disaster was the need to distinguish carefully between process safety and personal safety, and to manage these two types of safety differently. The authoritative Baker report following the accident defined these two types of safety as follows:[1]

> "*Personal* or *occupational* safety hazards give rise to incidents —
> such as slips, falls, and vehicle accidents — that primarily affect one
> individual worker for each occurrence. *Process* safety hazards give
> rise to major accidents involving the release of potentially dangerous
> materials, the release of energy (such as fires and explosions), or both.
> Process safety incidents can have catastrophic effects and can result
> in multiple injuries and fatalities, as well as substantial economic,
> property, and environmental damage. Process safety in a refinery
> involves the prevention of leaks, spills, equipment malfunctions, over-
> pressures, excessive temperatures, corrosion, metal fatigue, and other
> similar conditions."

Safety is commonly measured using workforce injury statistics (eg lost-time injuries, recordable injuries, first aids etc). A low injury rate is arguably evidence that conventional occupational hazards are being well managed, but such statistics imply nothing about how well *process* safety hazards are being managed. The problem is that catastrophic process safety incidents are, by their nature, rare and, even where process hazards are poorly managed, a facility may go for years without process-related injuries or fatalities. At the Texas City Refinery, process hazards were very poorly managed, and yet the injury rate was low, so low that employees were paid bonuses for their safety record.[2]

The problem is worse than this. An exclusive focus on personal injury statistics in hazardous industries is downright dangerous. It can lead companies to become complacent with respect to major hazards simply because they do not contribute to the injury statistics on an annual basis. That is what happened with BP at Texas City.

The Texas City accident was not the first time that this issue had been highlighted. Several previous inquiries into major accidents in gas plants and refineries had identified the way in which a focus on lost-time injuries had led to complacency with respect to process safety. These previous accident reports were well known to people at the Texas City Refinery, but they seemed unable to learn from them. Hence, the title of my previous book — *Failure to Learn*. We shall see that BP had still not properly learnt this lesson by the time of the Macondo accident.

Nor was BP alone in using injury statistics as a measure of overall safety. The petroleum industry had long opposed regulatory improvements for the Gulf of Mexico that might have strengthened the focus on process safety on the grounds that lost-time injury statistics had been steadily improving.[3] Even after the Macondo incident, the regulator continues to use injury statistics as its primary measure of safety.[4]

The term "process safety" originates in industries that *process* hazardous substances, such as petrochemical industries. Put simply, the issue in this context is "keeping it (the hazardous fluid) in the pipes". But the issue is broader than this. There are other hazardous industries, such as mining. Inquiries into major mine accidents have identified the same problem referred to here, namely, that companies have focused on personal injury statistics and ignored major accident risk, such as the risk of roof fall. It is important to understand that process safety risk is part of the broader category of major hazard risk. This is particularly important when we consider drilling, as will become apparent shortly.

There is one major hazard industry where the pattern identified above does not apply — the airline industry. In this context, major hazard risk refers to the risk of aircraft loss. No airline assumes that having good personal injury statistics implies anything about how well aircraft safety is being managed. The reason, no doubt, is that there is just too much at stake. When a passenger airliner crashes, hundreds of people are killed. The financial and reputational costs to the airline are enormous, and there is the real risk that passenger boycotts might threaten the very existence of the business. Moreover, unlike those killed in industrial accidents, many of the victims of plane crashes are likely to have been influential and/or to have influential relatives, which tends to magnify the costs and other consequences for the airline. For all of these reasons, airlines have developed distinctive ways of managing operational safety and would never make the mistake of using workforce injury statistics as a measure of aircraft safety. It is just as senseless in process industries as it is in the airline industry to assume that injury statistics tell us anything about how well major safety hazards are being managed.

BP in the Gulf of Mexico

Following the Texas City accident, BP as a whole accepted the importance of the distinction between personal and process safety and the need for a discrete focus on the latter. A considerable amount of work was subsequently done in parts of BP to improve process safety.

When it came to the Gulf of Mexico, the distinction was made, and personal safety was then joined with environment and health and referred to as "HSE".[5] In other words, the "safety" in HSE was quite explicitly intended to refer to personal safety only, not process safety.

This exclusion of process safety from the HSE portfolio was clearly understood by those involved. The senior health and safety manager for BP drilling operations in the Gulf of Mexico told various inquiries that his focus was on occupational safety, not process safety. He went on to explain that safety, for him, was about whether the action of pushing the button or turning the wrench posed risks specifically for the person carrying out this action. Whether pushing the button or turning the wrench was the right thing to do in the circumstances — whether it might lead to an explosion or a blowout — was not his concern.

That might have been reasonable had there been an equivalent group of specialists devoted to process or major hazard safety. But there wasn't.

The leadership team for BP's drilling operations prior to the accident is summarised Figure 5.1.

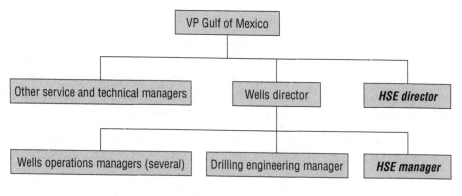

FIGURE 5.1: Drilling leadership team, 2009

The group of direct reports to the VP GoM (Vice President, Gulf of Mexico) Drilling contains an HSE director (in bold italics), while the direct reports to the "wells director" contains an HSE manager (in bold italics). This is an impressive positioning for HSE specialist staff, ensuring that HSE matters get a good hearing. But, remembering that HSE refers to personal safety, the question that this immediately raises is: what about process safety or major hazard risk management? Remarkably, there are no dedicated process safety positions at either level in this diagram. The distinction between personal and process safety had been made, and then, at least in this context, process safety had disappeared from the scene!

To return to the diagram, it will be noted that there is a drilling engineering manager at the lower level. This person was, in fact, a drilling engineering authority, meaning that he had responsibility for the maintenance of drilling engineering standards. From this point of view, at least one aspect of process safety is represented at this lower level.

But the engineering authority was not responsible for all aspects of process safety management. In particular, he was not responsible for whether or not workers were complying with procedures relevant to process safety. Some of the critical barrier failures in the Macondo incident involved failures by frontline workers, such as the failure to carry out the well integrity test properly and the failure to monitor flows of drilling fluid out of the well prior to departure. These were behavioural issues that fell outside the scope of the engineering authority.

The problem is that these behavioural process safety issues were likewise outside the scope of the HSE department. This meant, in particular, that the behavioural safety programs that BP ran[6] did not encompass the kind of worker behaviour that contributed to the Macondo disaster. There were, in fact, no specialist staff with a responsibility to ensure that workers complied with process safety procedures. This was a hugely significant gap in BP's safety framework and a hugely significant asymmetry in the way that it dealt with personal and process safety.*

The one-sided emphasis on personal safety had numerous other consequences. One such consequence was that the safety performance of contractors was evaluated using injury data,[7] leading the contractors to be much more focused on personal safety than process safety. Transocean, for example, was a stellar performer in terms of its injury statistics, but its well control discipline was inadequate.

Another dramatic demonstration of this one-sided approach to safety occurred on the day of the Macondo disaster. A group of VIPs from BP and Transocean was

---

* Readers of earlier drafts of this book suggested that this is not quite true, because line management was responsible for process safety behaviour. But line management was also responsible for personal safety. There was symmetry about the responsibilities of line management but asymmetry when it came to specialist support.

visiting the rig on a so-called "management visibility tour". They asked numerous questions about personal safety and none about process safety. The fact is that the errors and non-compliances which led directly to the incident were occurring as they walked around. Had the visitors asked any questions about how major accident risks were being managed, they would probably have identified those errors and non-compliances, thereby averting the accident. I shall discuss this VIP visit in more detail in Chapter 9.

It is important to give credit where credit is due. BP's commitment to personal safety was exemplary. A few days before the blowout, a rouseabout on the *Deepwater Horizon* received a slight injury to his leg from a load being lifted by a crane. The injury required only first aid treatment. BP managers discussed this in an email exchange. The well team leader suggested "a safety stand down tomorrow so we can get our act together". His boss replied: "Happy to take as much time as you think. 2 first aids and 2 drops in 2 weeks is worth a time out." Accordingly, the BP well team leader emailed a Transocean rig manager saying that it was "probably time to step back for an hour or two. Let's make sure the crew is engaged".[8] Where time is money, as it was for BP, to stop work in this way is a highly significant gesture. The fact that an injury requiring only first aid treatment could trigger such a response is an indication of how seriously BP took personal safety.

Transocean, too, took personal safety very seriously. It had a variety of safety programs that were all focused, perhaps inadvertently, on personal safety. In particular, Transocean had a policy known as "time out for safety". Here is how it was described at an inquiry:[9]

> "So if people see anything, whether they're in the same department, or they're walking by it, or they just see it, or they're looking for it [as when doing formal safety observations], they will take time out for safety."

Furthermore, Transocean monitored these time outs for safety and chose some of the more significant to make "I made a difference" awards. This is commendable as far as it goes. But these programs did not in practice cover major hazards and, on the day of the accident, despite numerous troubling anomalies, no one thought that it might be appropriate to stop the job or to take time out for safety.[10]

Well control incidents and safety

Let us focus this discussion on the most significant process safety event for a drilling rig — a blowout. Consider the following passage from an introductory text:[11]

> "Before a well blows out, it kicks. A kick is the entry of enough formation fluids [oil and gas] into the well bore so ... [as to create an upward] pressure in the well. If crew members fail to recognize that the well has kicked and do not take proper steps to control it [by sealing the well], it can blow out ... The key to preventing blowouts is recognizing and controlling kicks before they become blowouts."

A kick, then, is a precursor to a blowout and, as such, is a highly significant safety issue. But because of the focus on personal safety, well control incidents (as they are also called) were not recognised as safety issues and were not reported through the safety reporting system.[12] This was a matter of policy. A Transocean official put it quite bluntly: "We don't recognise well control as a safety issue."[13]

Was it perhaps recognised, more specifically, as a *process* safety issue? According to BP's managers, it was not. This raises the following question. If well control incidents, though the precursors to a blowout, were not considered to be process safety events, just what did process safety mean in the BP drilling environment. The answer is: very little. I shall demonstrate this in more detail in Chapter 6.

Concluding comments

BP distinguished carefully between process and personal safety and then proceeded to focus heavily on personal safety — almost to the exclusion of process safety, particularly in drilling.

BP's own judgment in 2008 was that process safety was poorly understood in its Gulf of Mexico operations, not just in drilling, but in production as well:[14]

> "As we have started to more deeply investigate process safety incidents, it's become apparent that process safety major hazards and risks are not fully understood by engineering or line operating personnel. Insufficient awareness is leading to missed signals that precede incidents and response after incidents; both of which increases the potential for, and severity of, process safety related incidents."

In the case of drilling, the problem, as we have seen, was embedded in the organisational structure. The management team for drilling included two high-level personal safety managers, but no one with a dedicated focus on process safety. This provides some insight into the otherwise puzzling insistence by BP managers after the Macondo accident that safety was never sacrificed in order to achieve cost savings.[15] In making such claims, they were referring to *personal* safety and, given the company focus on personal safety, their claims are quite plausible.

Let us return, finally, to some of the defences that failed. Consider the Macondo engineering team members. They were right in thinking that their design decisions did not introduce additional personal safety risks. Those decisions *did* have implications for process safety, but process safety was quite remote from their thinking. It was just not on their radar. This chapter goes some way towards explaining why.

This analysis has direct relevance to two other defence failures — the failure of the well integrity test and the failure to monitor the well in the final stages before departure. These failures involved errors and violations by employees in the hours immediately before the blowout. The behaviour of these people was not subject to any scrutiny or verification, and it was not recognised by anyone that their behaviour had implications for major hazard safety. Similarly, it was the behaviour of operators that triggered the Texas City accident, but their behaviour was not seen as relevant to safety because of a general blindness to process safety risk.

One solution to this problem would be for BP to extend the behaviour safety programs run by HSE specialist staff to cover behaviour that is relevant to process safety, such as mud monitoring. If behavioural observations had been made on the activities of the rig crew in the final hours before the blowout, a number of their errors and violations might have come to light. Such an extension would require a re-definition of the responsibilities of HSE staff to include at least some aspects of process safety. The point is that the behavioural approach is just as applicable to process safety as it is to personal safety, and auditing and monitoring activities should cover both. This conclusion has relevance way beyond BP. One of the criticisms that has been levelled at behavioural safety generally is that it ignores process safety.[16] It is vital that behavioural safety programs face and overcome this criticism.

Endnotes

1   Baker et al, 2007, p x.

2   Sources for all of these claims about the Texas City Refinery accident are provided in Hopkins, 2008.

3   H Ryggvik, "Statistical contradictions, BBS and under-reporting: a comparative perspective on the Norwegian and US offshore sectors", p 2, unpublished paper; Federal Register, vol 79, no. 199, 15 October 2010, Rules and Regulations, p 63612.

4   Federal Register, vol 75, no. 199, 15 October 2010, Rules and Regulations, p 63635.

5   For simplicity, I omit "security" from HSSE here and refer only to HSE.

6   DWI, 26 May, Tink, p 343.

7   DWI, 26 May, pp 357, 358, 364, 365.

8   BOEMRE, pp 83, 84.

9   DWI, 26 May, p 446.

10   BOEMRE, p 190. Transocean's safety policies are described in BOEMRE (pp 185–188).

11   Diener, 1999, p 1.

12   DWI, 9 December, pm, p 100.

13   DWI, 9 December, pm, Caducci, pp 80, 81.

14   CCR, pp 243, 244.

15   See, for example, DWI, 22 July, Guide, p 61.

16   Hopkins, 2006.

CHAPTER 6

CHOOSING THE RIGHT MEASURES AND MAKING THEM MATTER

There is an old adage that what gets measured gets managed. This is not quite true. It is only true if the measures are made to matter. So there are really two steps to ensuring that something is managed well: first, devising the appropriate measures; and second, making those measures matter. To come to the point, if major hazards are to be managed effectively, we must first devise appropriate indicators and then make those indicators matter. That is what this chapter is about. It will show that BP made laudable efforts to develop process safety indicators and to make them matter by including them in performance agreements. This meant that performance in relation to process safety indicators would directly affect financial bonuses. However, the world of drilling remained untouched by these efforts. As a result — and this is the central argument of this chapter — for drilling operations in the Gulf of Mexico, the cost pressures inherent in performance agreements were unconstrained by any concern for major hazard safety.

Process safety indicators

As noted in Chapter 5, one of main lessons coming out of the Texas City Refinery disaster was the need for a separate focus on process safety, as opposed to personal safety. This means, in particular, the need to develop process safety indicators. The Baker report recommended that BP adopt a composite process safety indicator consisting of the number of fires, explosions, loss of containment events, and process-related injuries. The US Centre for Chemical Process Safety subsequently recommended that the chemical industry as a whole adopt such a measure.

Where a site is experiencing numerous fires and loss of containment incidents, as Texas City was, such a measure is a useful indicator of how well process safety is being managed, in the sense that a reduction in the number of such incidents implies an improvement in process safety management. At some sites, however, the number of fires and loss of containment incidents will already be so low that such figures cannot be used to monitor changes in the effectiveness of process safety management. To make the point concretely, if there is one loss of containment event in one year but two in the next, it cannot be assumed that the safety management system has deteriorated. Although this is a doubling, or an increase of 100%, the numbers are too small to be statistically significant. The increase may simply be a matter of chance. In contrast, if the numbers went from 100 to 200 (the same percentage increase), we would certainly want to infer that the situation had deteriorated.

Where the numbers are too low to be able to identify trends, an alternative approach to measuring process safety is needed. That approach is to identify the barriers, that is, defences or controls, that are supposed to be in place to prevent a major accident event, and to measure how well those controls are performing. To give a simple example: if safety depends in part on pressure relief valves opening when required, then what is needed is some measure of how well they are functioning. Or a different kind of example: if one of the controls on which safety depends is a requirement that operators stay within predetermined operating limits, then we need to measure the extent to which they are exceeding those limits.

Indicators of the first type (numbers of gas releases and fires) are sometimes called "lagging indicators", while measures like deviations from safe operating limits are sometimes referred to as "leading indicators". The US Chemical Safety Board recommended that the American Petroleum Institute (API) develop a set of such leading and lagging indicators.[1] The Institute did just that and finally published *Recommended Practice 754: Process Safety Performance Indicators for the Refining and Petrochemical Industries* in April 2010 — coincidentally, the month of the Macondo accident.

API 754 defines a process safety pyramid, analogous to the familiar personal safety pyramid, or triangle, or iceberg (see Figure 6.1).

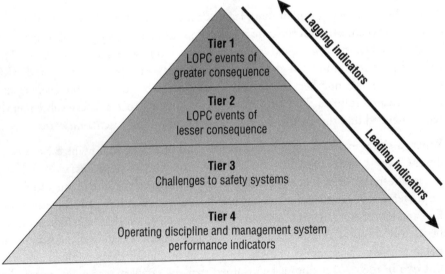

FIGURE 6.1: API 754 process safety indicator pyramid

Simplifying somewhat, Tier 1 is defined as follows:

(1) any loss of primary containment (LOPC), *regardless of size*, which has significant consequences, such as a lost-time injury or fire; or

(2) any loss of primary containment *greater than a certain threshold size*, even though there may be no consequences.

Since most releases have no immediately harmful consequences, it is the second category that is likely to contribute most to the indicator. The threshold size mentioned in this second category depends on the kind of material involved. For example, for a flammable gas, the threshold is 500 kg in any one hour, while the threshold for oil[2] is 2,000 kg per hour — four times as much. The difference arises because, in the API's view, the latter types of release are "events with lesser consequences".[3] In other words, the standard is slanted towards gas releases as the most serious process safety events. This point will become relevant later in this chapter.

Tier 2 is defined in similar terms, but with smaller thresholds.

A Tier 3 event is defined as one that "represents a challenge to the barrier system that progressed along the path to harm but is stopped short of a Tier 1 or Tier 2 LOPC". For example:

- an excursion from safe operating limits;
- test results outside acceptable limits;
- a demand on a safety system, such as the lifting of a pressure relief valve.

Tier 4 refers to measures of process safety management system activities, such as:

- process hazard evaluations completed on time;
- action items closed on time;
- training completed on schedule;
- procedures current and accurate;
- work permit compliance.

Where Tier 1 or Tier 2 events are occurring with sufficient frequency to be able to compute a rate, the focus must be at this level and the aim must be to drive the rate downwards. Where the number of loss of containment events is too small to be able to compute a meaningful rate, the focus shifts to Tier 3 and Tier 4. This will often be the situation at specific sites. But for some large sites, such as the Texas City Refinery, and for large companies and whole industries, the number of loss of containment events will be large enough to keep the focus at this level.

In the years following the Texas City accident, BP developed various process safety indicators, central among them being loss of containment events. The data were carefully analysed at corporate headquarters and presented in a uniform manner that allowed comparisons across the company.[4] In 2010, BP adopted the API definitions described above, with an emphasis on Tier 1 and Tier 2 loss of containment events. (The distinction between loss of primary containment (LOPC) and loss of containment (LOC) is not entirely clear.[5] For present purposes, I shall use the terms interchangeably.)

Making process safety indicators matter

The inquiries following the Texas City accident were very clear that it was not enough simply to develop process safety indicators. They had to be made to matter, by including them in pay systems. So, the Baker Panel recommended that:[6]

> "… a significant proportion of total compensation of refining line managers and supervisors [should be] contingent on satisfactorily meeting process safety performance goals …"

The reasoning was simple. If pay systems emphasise production and cost-reduction targets without also specifying process safety targets, process safety will suffer. As Bergin bluntly remarks: "Managers did not act to prevent Texas City because every incentive and potential penalty they faced told them not to."[7]

But BP was slow to implement this recommendation. The company appointed an "independent expert" to report annually on progress towards implementation of the Baker Panel recommendations, and his second report states:[8]

> "The 2008 variable pay plan objective for Refining included process safety metrics, but performance scores were not awarded for any category of objectives or for any individual objective. As a result the independent expert could not confirm whether a significant portion of the resulting payouts under the plan was based on satisfactorily meeting the process safety goals and objectives recommended by the Baker Panel."

This is a somewhat obscure statement. A year later, the independent expert is rather more forceful:[9]

> "With respect to leading and lagging process safety indicators, additional steps are required to develop performance targets for each indicator. BP must hold line management accountable for meeting at least these minimum targets."

Clearly, in 2009, refinery managers were still not being held financially accountable for process safety.

In 2010, nothing had changed.[10] In 2011, process safety metrics, together with specific targets, were finally included in performance contracts of US refinery managers, although the details have not been made public.[11] It had taken BP four years to implement this particular recommendation of the Baker Panel.

The ubiquity of cost pressures in the Macondo context

In order to understand the importance of making process safety measures matter for drilling operations, we need some understanding of just how powerful and ubiquitous cost pressures were in the drilling context.

According to one senior manager, "every conversation, every decision has some cost factor". That's the way it must be for every company in business.[12] He was provided with an update on drilling costs every day, he said.[13] The Macondo well team leader echoed this. The team kept track of costs on a daily basis and compiled a cumulative total so that they were always aware of where they stood in relation to authorised expenditure. The well team leader noted that there was a weekly meeting about costs and that there was a large technical group of cost analysts and cost engineers that kept track of costs.[14]

The Gulf of Mexico drilling organisation engaged in regular benchmarking (comparison) exercises against BP drilling organisations in other parts of the world, and against other companies. A company called Rushmore collected data from the drilling industry generally (on such things as days per 10,000 ft of well drilled), and fed this information back to all contributors so that they could see in which quartile they fell. Of course, everyone wants to be in the top quartile but, by definition, only 25% can. These comparisons therefore magnified the pressure to reduce costs.

One other activity that put pressure on drilling teams to work as rapidly as possible was the idea of a technical limit.[15] Based on historical data, BP had identified the fastest times for various well-drilling operations.[16] Prior to drilling each well, the team would hold an offsite "technical limit meeting" to "drill the well on paper". This involved identifying in detail each step of the drilling operation for a particular well. Then, knowing the best achieved times for each step, they could calculate the best achievable time for drilling this particular well — the technical limit. Inevitably, drilling will fall behind this timetable, giving rise to a constant pressure to drill faster.

BP was committed to creating an "every dollar counts culture", which meant that cost control could go to extraordinary lengths. The head of drilling operations for the Gulf of Mexico was twice asked to explain to his boss why he was using a brand of coffee at his headquarters in Houston that was costing $70 a month more than an alternative brand![17]

Performance agreements

One of the most powerful ways in which cost pressure operated was via the performance agreements that were made at every level of management. The goals of the business unit leader for the Gulf of Mexico were set in consultation with his boss, the global head of exploration and production. These goals were then cascaded downwards, meaning that the goals of direct reports were designed to support the goals of the boss, and so on down the line. The goals of the most senior executives included various numerical targets, and these numerical targets were cascaded downwards, wherever lower-level managers had the capacity to influence the numbers. Below that, goals were stated in qualitative rather than quantitative terms.

What is critical about these performance agreements is that staff were paid bonuses depending on how well they performed with respect to these agreements. According to Bergin, "for senior drilling personnel, annual bonuses could add over $100,000 to salaries of around $200,000".[18] Some measures included "stretch targets" which, if met, attracted an even higher bonus. This was indeed a powerful incentive system, designed to align personal and corporate goals.

Not surprisingly, commercial goals were prominent in these performance agreements. One important measure was speed of drilling (days per 10,000 ft). The impact on well site leaders can be seen in a request that one of them made to the driller to "bump it up", that is, increase the speed of drilling. The driller's judgment would have been that they were drilling as fast as they could in the prevailing geological circumstances. Nevertheless, the company man wanted him to drill faster. He obeyed and, within days, there was trouble. According to a witness, "we lost circulation. We blew the bottom out of the well".[19] Bergin notes that "because drilling too fast was dangerous, other companies were not usually in the practice of focusing on such a metric". He quotes one BP senior executive as admitting that "we stumbled into incentivising people the wrong way".

The inquiry by the regulator discovered another way that these pressures affected behaviour. It noted that, of 13 employees whose performance evaluations it had examined, 12 had documented ways in which they had saved the company large sums of money. One had put together a spreadsheet showing how he had saved the company $490,000.[20]

Interestingly, "[BP] engineers had their bonuses and promotional prospects linked to drilling efficiency, so their incentive was to press ahead quickly and to spend as little as possible".[21] This was clearly evident in the behaviour of the Macondo engineers for whom, as we saw, cost and schedule were enormously important. It is obvious that the cost and time pressures that BP had created for its engineers potentially undermined their commitment to engineering excellence.

It is worth considering the particular case of BP's engineering authorities in this context. These people are, in effect, the custodians of BP's engineering standards. Where an operations (ie line) manager seeks to deviate from a standard, the engineering authority can authorise the deviation if the risk is judged to be acceptable. Being an engineering authority is not a full-time activity. Engineering authorities are selected based on their expertise and are not located at predetermined places in the organisational structure. They may, in fact, be line managers. But the performance agreements of line managers highlight cost-reduction targets. In principle, there would seem to be a particular conflict of interest here.

The place of safety in performance agreements

Given that commercial considerations are so centrally embedded in the performance agreements of line managers and engineers, the question arises as to whether there were any safety requirements contained in these agreements that might serve to constrain, temper or balance these cost imperatives.

BP had long included indicators of personal safety in its performance agreements, in particular, recordable injury frequency and days-away-from-work case frequency.[22] Targets were set and bonuses were directly influenced by whether or not these targets were reached. This was not just Gulf of Mexico practice; it was company-wide. It resulted in a remarkable focus on personal injury hazards in the Gulf of Mexico, as was demonstrated in Chapter 5.

But what of process safety? BP recognised the need for process safety indicators and, following the Texas City accident, it had tried to develop relevant indicators. There was, however, a degree of confusion about these efforts.

For some time, the company had treated the number of oil spills as a process safety indicator. In its 2009 annual review, for example, this was the only indicator of process safety that was mentioned. Even after the Macondo accident, BP stated in its submission to the National Academy of Engineers that "oil spill data is a process safety metric".

However, while an oil spill is certainly an environmental issue, its relevance to process safety is far less clear. Oil is not volatile and so does not readily generate an explosive mixture in the way that a gas release does. In short, while oil burns, it does not explode. An oil spill, therefore, is far less dangerous than a gas release.[23] BP drillers were very concerned about oil spills (for instance, from hydraulic hoses) precisely because the number of oil spills was a performance indicator that mattered. But such events had little catastrophic potential.

Interestingly, BP drillers distinguished between oil leaks and oil spills, and both were tracked. If a release was contained on deck, it was a leak; if it reached the ocean, it became something more serious — a spill. This distinction makes perfect sense from an environmental point of view — a spill into the ocean is more polluting than one that is contained on deck. But the distinction makes little sense from a process safety point of view — oil on water is difficult to ignite and, from this point of view, it is less dangerous than a spill on deck. In summary, while the number of oil spills is an important environmental indicator, it is not a good process safety indicator.

BP seems belatedly to have recognised this. In its 2010 annual report, it states:[24]

> "BP is progressively moving towards [loss of primary containment] as one of the key indicators for process safety, as we believe it provides a more comprehensive and better performance indicator of the safety and integrity of our facilities than oil spills alone."

So it was that, in 2010, BP adopted the API 754 definitions of loss of primary containment (which emphasise gas releases) and began including loss of primary containment (so defined) in remuneration agreements of its most senior managers.[25] This was the situation in the Gulf of Mexico at the time of the Macondo accident.

The lack of relevance of the loss of containment indicator to drilling

Unfortunately, BP's attempt to do the right thing was fundamentally flawed. API 754 is applicable to any industry where a loss of containment has the potential to cause serious harm.[26] It specifically applies to the refining and petrochemical industries and it is potentially relevant to upstream oil and gas *production*, but *drilling* is a different matter. I shall argue here that loss of containment is *not* a significant indicator of how well major hazards on a drilling rig are being managed.

Consider, again, what makes loss of containment events significant. In much of the petroleum industry, a loss of containment of flammable gas or volatile hydrocarbon liquid is an event that, in certain circumstances, can result in an explosion, or a catastrophic jet fire, or a boiling liquid expanding vapour explosion (BLEVE). In other words, such loss of containment events are precursors to a major accident. It follows that, by reducing the number of such events, the risk of a major accident event can be reduced.

Now consider the drilling industry. Gas can be and is released from wells during the drilling process and can reach dangerous levels on a rig. Speaking about the gas alerts on the *Deepwater Horizon*, one witness said:[27]

> "... we had gotten them so frequently that I had actually become somewhat immune to them. I'd get to the point where I didn't even hear them anymore because we were getting gas back continuously. It was a constant fight. When the level reached 200, that's the cut-off for all chipping, welding and grinding and other outside hot work. That's when I start concerning myself with gas levels ... [That's when] I don't need to be making sparks anywhere, of any kind. So at that point is when I really start paying attention to gas levels."

It is apparent from this account that gas releases during well-drilling operations were not normally regarded as significant. Nor were they treated as reportable loss of containment events. The gas referred to is largely "drill gas" or "vent gas" that is routinely generated in some wells as drilling progresses, especially when drilling through shale. It is normally vented to the atmosphere.[28] Most importantly, it is not a precursor to a blowout. Hence, even if such releases were treated as reportable loss of containment events, reducing the number of such events would not necessarily reduce the risk of a blowout.

Vent gas does not have the catastrophic potential of a blowout, but it is a hazard in its own right. Unfortunately, the API standard is of no use in this context. The standard depends on the ability to estimate the *weight* of gas released, and it is unlikely that realistic estimates could be made of the weight of vent gas released. However, what *can* be measured is the number of occasions on which vent gas reaches dangerous *concentrations*. This would be an entirely different indicator. It is desirable that such an indicator be developed. The regulator was aware of the problem of vent gas on the *Deepwater Horizon* and had requested that the drilling "proceed with caution". A relevant indicator would greatly assist with the management of this hazard.

Chapter

6

Kicks

So what might sensibly be used an as indicator of blowout risk in drilling? If blowouts were occurring sufficiently often to be able talk about a rate that could be driven downwards, then the blowout rate itself would be an appropriate indicator of blowout risk. However, according to a study by the regulator, there were 39 blowouts in the Gulf of Mexico in a 15-year period from 1992 to 2006, that is, an average of between two and three per year.[29] This is too small a number to be useful.

Consider, therefore, the immediate precursor to a blowout, namely, a well kick or a well control incident (these terms are used interchangeably). As noted in Chapter 5, a well kick can occur when drilling through oil and gas sands. Sometimes the pressure in those sands is great enough to overcome the weight of the drilling fluid, and oil and gas may begin to enter the well bore and make its way upwards. This is a kick. Unless operators control the kick in some way, it can develop into a blowout. Kicks are more numerous than blowouts, and it is widely recognised that reducing the number of kicks reduces the risk of blowout. Regulators in some parts of the world routinely collect and publish data on numbers of kicks.[30] For any one well, the number of kicks may be too small to serve as a useful indicator, but the number per company per year is something that companies could usefully compute and seek to drive downwards.

One consideration when introducing new indicators, especially if they are indicators that matter, is the ease with which they can be manipulated. Where measures are made to matter, the first response is to try to *manage the measure*. The simplest strategy is to discourage reporting, but there are also clever classification games that can be played to minimise the figures. Lost-time injury statistics, for example, suffer from this kind of manipulation.[31] Even losses of containment can be manipulated. The weight of a release must be calculated from pressure, duration and size of the hole, all of which must be estimated, which leaves plenty of room for data manipulation. A kick, however, is a relatively unambiguous event which is not easily suppressed. The number of kicks is therefore a reasonably robust indicator from this point of view.

Let us pause for a moment to consider the problem of under-reporting that often occurs when a measure such as loss of containment is made to matter. This is a very real problem. Fortunately, there is a solution, which involves fine-tuning the incentive arrangements. Senior managers are the ones who are in a position to drive down rates of loss of containment, or any other indicator that matters, by using the management tools at their disposal. They must therefore be provided with incentives to do so. However, for many indicators (for example, losses of containment), we may be relying on frontline workers to report occurrences; it follows that they must have an incentive to do so. This means, first, that their remuneration must not be dependent on driving down the relevant rate, and second, that they should be provided with a positive incentive to report. Where the occurrences of interest are well defined, such as a loss of containment, this might be achieved by offering a small financial reward for each occurrence that is reported. The overall effect of these incentive arrangements will be to drive reporting up, while simultaneously driving the real occurrence rate down.

Returning to the question of kicks, it is sometimes argued that wells differ in complexity and hence propensity to kick, and that any indicator based simply on the number of kicks would therefore be misleading. This may be so. But there are ways in which levels of complexity can be taken into account so that valid comparisons may be made.[32] This is clearly the kind of refinement that needs to be made as systems of measurement become more mature.

Unfortunately, BP had not recognised the importance of using the number of kicks as an indicator of blowout risk prior to the Macondo event. Data on the number of kicks were recorded, but this was not a measure that mattered. Trend data on kicks were not put in front of the Gulf of Mexico management team. Nor did performance agreements set targets for a reduction in the number of kicks.

The problem is that BP had not given any thought to how it might transfer to the drilling environment the heightened awareness of process safety generated by the Texas City accident. A senior BP executive acknowledged after the accident that, in his mind, process safety referred to production platforms, while for drilling rigs, the issue was simply safety, by which he meant personal safety. In fact, while numerical process safety targets were included in the performance agreements of the executives responsible for production, there were no such targets in the performance agreements for drilling executives.[33] In this way, process safety simply disappeared from view when it came to drilling.

Chapter

6

Other indicators of blowout risk

Various other potential indicators of blowout risk became apparent during the inquiries after the Macondo accident.[34]

Kick response times

Blowout prevention relies on drillers recognising kicks as soon as possible after they have occurred, and taking corrective action, such as closing off the well. On the night of the Macondo blowout, drillers took about 40 minutes to recognise that a kick had occurred, by which time it was too late. A little over a month earlier, the *Deepwater Horizon* experienced another kick which went unnoticed for 33 minutes. Subsequent analysis indicted that it should have been recognised much earlier.[35] One can therefore easily imagine an indicator based on response time to kicks, which would be relevant at a company or industry level, if not at the level of individual wells. The data are all recorded automatically so, as before, this would be a reasonably robust indicator. Interestingly, BP and Transocean did unannounced tests of response time, perhaps once a week. These tests involved simulating a kick and seeing how long it took crews to recognise and respond to the changed circumstances. This could also serve as the basis for an indicator of how well blowout risk is being managed.

Cementing failures

Another potential indicator of blowout risk is the number of cementing failures. The Macondo blowout was initiated by an unrecognised cementing failure. Moreover, there had been two previous cementing failures higher up the well. The regulator study referred to earlier found that, of the 39 blowouts in the 15-year period under consideration, 18 had been initiated by cementing failures. Cement failure is therefore a precursor event, and driving down the rate of cement failures would be desirable from a safety point of view, as well as being commercially desirable.

Hazard-specific indicators

A general point emerges from this discussion: process safety indicators need to be chosen in light of the major hazard that is to be managed. One petroleum company that I have studied identified its most worrying major accident scenario as a road tanker accident resulting in fire or explosion. It was monitoring driver behaviour using data recorders, and decided to use these data to identify precursor situations, that is, situations of heightened risk. The first idea was to focus on the number of occasions on which drivers exceeded the speed limit. However, analysis revealed that some of the most dangerous situations occurred at speeds that were lower than the limit and, conversely, there were situations where exceeding the speed limit did not significantly increase the risk of an accident. It was then realised that, when drivers were forced to brake harder than usual, they were not as much in control of the situation as was desirable. These "hard brakes" were therefore precursor events, worth monitoring, studying and driving down.

Again, a collision between vessels at sea, or between a vessel and a platform, could be a major accident event. The Norwegian offshore regulator collects data on the number of occasions on which vessels are on a collision course. Alternatively, one might monitor occasions on which vessels are closer to each other, or to a platform, than they should be. Such an event can be described as a "breakdown of separation". This is the most important indicator of safety used by air traffic control around the world. Breakdowns of separation are precursor events that can be monitored and driven downwards. The general point, then, is that, in the petroleum industry, loss of containment is not always the most appropriate indicator of major hazard risk. Indicators need to be tailored to specific major accident events. This is particularly true for blowouts.

Precursor indicators versus other indicators of risk

The attentive reader will note that this discussion has been largely about precursor events, the equivalent of the Tier 1 and Tier 2 indicators in the API triangle for the refining and petrochemical industries (Figure 6.1). But there are also circumstances in which we need to consider more remote indicators of risk, such as the Tier 3 and Tier 4 indicators. This is just as true in the drilling industry and other major hazard industries as it is for the refining and petrochemical industries. Companies and business units need to pay attention to these more remote indicators when they do not have large enough numbers of precursor events to be able to construct meaningful indicators.

However, there are good reasons to concentrate on the precursor events when we are developing measures for inclusion in the performance agreements of senior managers. Appropriate precursor indicators measure risk in a direct and obvious way. In turn, they encourage senior managers to think harder about how to drive risk down. Those managers may decide that the best way is to develop a suite of Tier 3 and Tier 4 indicators tailored to their own environment, or they may opt for other tactics, such as better auditing or closer supervision. The precursor event indicator leaves managers free to work out the best risk reduction strategies in their particular environment, while maintaining the pressure on them to do just that.

Chapter

6

There is another reason to focus at the top end of the pyramid when constructing indicators for inclusion in performance agreements. Tier 4 indicators, such as the number of audit recommendations closed out on time, rapidly lead to perverse outcomes if they become measures that matter. If close-out rates are made to affect bonuses, managers may increase the *quantity* of close-outs by sacrificing their *quality*. As a result, they may be able to meet whatever close-out targets are set, without additional resources, but without necessarily improving safety. This is not dishonesty, simply pragmatism. It is a reasonable hypothesis that the more causally remote the indicator is from the outcome of concern, the greater the opportunities for perverse outcomes of this nature.

BP's response

With these cautionary observations in mind, let us consider finally the set of indicators that BP has developed since the Macondo incident to assist with the management of blowout risk:[36]

- well control (kick) and/or blowout preventer activation events;
- well control incident investigations — overdue actions;
- approved deviations from engineering technical practices;

- rig safety critical equipment failures — overdue actions;
- the number of wells with sustained casing pressure;
- the number of wells with failed sub-surface safety valves or down-hole safety valves; and
- the number of BP Macondo incident investigation report recommendations implemented.

The first of these is essentially the kick indicator recommended earlier. The others are a judicious mixture of Tier 1 to Tier 4 indicators that BP thinks will help it to manage the risk of blowout most effectively. The crucial question is: which, if any, of these indicators will become measures that matter, in the sense of affecting remuneration. BP has not made this information public.

The only comment that I wish to make on this set of indicators concerns the third item, approved deviations from engineering technical practices — presumably, the fewer the better. There are two reasons why engineering authorities might approve deviations. The first is when the standards are not in fact appropriate or necessary in the circumstances. If deviations are being approved for this reason, then the use of the proposed indicator will drive improvements in the standards, because the more carefully designed the standards are, the fewer will be the situations for which they are seen to be inappropriate. The second reason why engineering authorities might approve a deviation is that line managers are seeking a relaxation of a standard for commercial reasons, and are arguing that the increase in risk is insignificant or at least reasonable in the circumstances. This puts engineering authorities in a difficult position. The problem is that, although in any one case it may be true that the deviation does not significantly increase the risk, if such authorisations become the norm, the associated risks will creep imperceptibly upwards. The proposed indicator helps to control this process and strengthens the will of the approver to resist commercial pressures. Furthermore, this is a relatively robust indicator, in the sense that authorisation is a discrete event and hence the number of authorisations is difficult to fudge. (Of course, along with most other indicators, it can be falsified, but that is another issue altogether.) For this reason, it might well be appropriate to make this a measure that matters by specifying targets in performance agreements. While on this subject, a related indicator is the number of authorised safety system bypasses. This too is an indicator that should be made to matter.

Concluding remarks

BP did the right thing in trying to construct indicators of process safety and include them in performance agreements. But it failed to translate the idea of process safety into the drilling context. This meant that, for the Macondo team, there was no impetus to reduce the risk of blowout. This provides further insight into the team's failure to think carefully about the safety of what it was doing.

Suppose we ask the following question: given that a major accident was to occur in BP's Gulf of Mexico operations, why did it occur on a drilling rig and not a production platform? This chapter suggests a possible answer. The indicator of major hazard risk that BP had developed and had included in performance agreements was relevant to production platforms, but not drilling rigs. It was therefore effective in drawing attention to major hazard risk on production platforms, but not on drilling rigs.

I concur with the penultimate paragraph of Tom Bergin's book on BP, which includes the following words:[37]

> "The extent to which a company is a good social citizen is less a function of its managers' moral compass than of ... the incentives given by them to employees. If they develop badly thought-out incentives and enforce them blindly, there will be unintended consequences, something the financial sector has illustrated on a grand scale in recent years."

Chapter

6

Endnotes

1   CSB, 2007, p 212. The lead/lag terminology is somewhat confusing and its use will be minimised here. See Hopkins, 2009a.

2   Strictly speaking, this threshold is for substances with a flashpoint of greater than 60°C. Furthermore, it only counts if the substance is released at a temperature greater than its flashpoint.

3   API 754, p 12.

4   "HSE and operations integrity reports" (BP's so-called "orange books"). See *Fourth annual report of the independent expert*, March 2011, p 28, available on the BP website.

5   The concept of *primary* containment creates some difficulties. Suppose a container is over-pressured and pressure relief valves lift, releasing flammable gas. But suppose further that this gas is contained via a secondary containment system and released to the atmosphere through a flare, as combustion products only. Logically, this sequence of events amounts to a loss of primary containment of a flammable material, with containment and neutralisation by the secondary containment system. It appears that this is the view of the standard writers when they say (at para 6.1): "Tier 2 PSEs, even those that have been contained by secondary systems, indicate barrier system weaknesses that may be potential precursors of future, more significant incidents." However, some commentators argue that the scenario just described is not an LOPC.

6   Baker et al, p 251.

7   Bergin, 2011, p 85.

8   *Second annual report of the independent expert*, March 2009, p 3.

9   *Third annual report of the independent expert*, March 2010, p 20.

10 *Fourth annual report of the independent expert*, March 2011, p 29.

11   *Fifth annual report of the independent expert*, April 2012, p 21.

12   DWI, 26 August, Sims, p 145.

13   DWI, 26 August, Sims, p189.

14   DWI, 7 October, Guide, pp 161, 162.

15   CCR, p 247.

16   CCR, p 247.

17   Personal communication.

18   This section draws on Bergin, 2011, pp 126, 127.

19   DWI, 23 July, Williams, pp 36, 37.

20   DWI, 7 October, p 148.

21   Bergin, 2011, p 153.

22   See BP annual reports.

23   This is fundamental to the definitions of Tier 1 and Tier 2 events in API 754, as discussed earlier.

24   At p 12. This statement is confusing. An oil spill is indeed a measure of integrity — it is a loss of containment, loosely defined. But it is not a measure of process safety. If the argument in the text is accepted, LOPC (as defined in API 754) should replace the number of oil spills, not augment it, as an indicator of process safety.

25   BP annual reports for 2009, p 84; 2010, p 114; 2011, p 140.

26   Section 1.2.

27   DWI, 23 July, Williams, pp 8, 9.

28   I am indebted to David Pritchard for this account.

29   Izon et al, 2007.

30   For example, Norway; see Skogdalen et al, 2011. Also Australia; see www.nopsa.gov.au/document/Charts%20-%20Quarterly%20Key%20Performance%20Indicators%20June%202011.pdf.

31   Hopkins, 2008, pp 85, 86.

32   D Pritchard and K Lacy, "Deepwater well complexity — the new domain", working paper for Deepwater Horizon Study Group, January 2011.

33   Personal communication.

34   A much fuller discussion of this topic can be found in Skogdalen et al, 2011.

35   BP, 2010, p 107; see also BP, 2011, p 9.

36   BP, 2011, p 51.

37   Bergen, 2011, p 267.

CHAPTER 7

ORGANISATIONAL STRUCTURE

The Macondo accident was initiated by poor engineering decision-making that culminated in a declaration that the well had been successfully cemented, when it fact it had not. We have already examined some of the organisational factors that undermined the quality of engineering decision-making, such as the failure of BP to provide appropriate financial incentives. Another contributing factor was BP's organisational structure which, as we shall see, subordinated engineers to line managers. This chapter examines the issue and shows how BP was seeking to improve its organisational structure at the time of the blowout. The argument will be that the improvement came too late to prevent disaster.

The issues

Before examining the matter in the context of the Macondo accident, it will be useful to develop some of the issues in a more abstract way. Large corporations often consist of a series of business units which, in turn, may be made up of sub-business units, and so on. These units at various levels are often described as assets, and the term "asset" is used interchangeably with business or sub-business unit here. Asset managers are accountable for the business performance of their assets. The assets may require the services of various kinds of specialists, most relevantly in the present context, engineers. There are two potential reporting lines for engineers working for a particular asset or business unit: they may report to the asset manager, or they may report to a more senior engineer who is not a part of that particular asset. The more senior engineer may report to the asset manager at the next level up or to a more senior engineer, and so on. This ancillary engineering line must, at some point, report to a person who is accountable for business performance, the ultimate possibility being that the engineering line goes all the way to the CEO. This range of possibilities is represented in Figures 7.1 to 7.3. Solid lines in these diagrams represent lines of formal accountability; dotted lines refer to the provision of engineering services to assets.

The distinction between asset managers and engineering (or other specialist activities) is usually described as a distinction between line and function, that is, between *line* management and specialists who serve a particular *function*. Using this language, we can say that the models described in Figures 7.1 to 7.3 differ in that line and function come together at progressively higher levels of the organisation. Where hierarchies of specialist authority go all the way to the top, the organisation is sometimes described as a functional organisation.

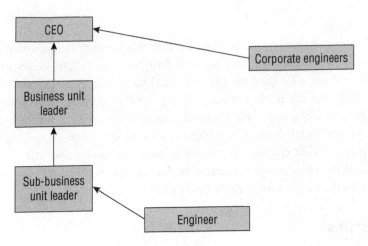

FIGURE 7.1: Base-level engineer reports to sub-business unit leader — a "decentralised" organisation

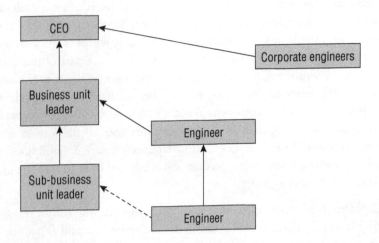

FIGURE 7.2: Base-level engineer reports to more senior engineer

Note that, even where engineers report to the lowest-level asset managers, the corporation may have corporate engineers reporting at a high level (as in Figure 7.1), but these people exercise no direct control over lower-level engineers and have other responsibilities, such as standard setting.

These different models have different consequences for decision-making. Consider a situation where a base-level asset engineer is proposing the best engineering practice, while the base-level asset manager is willing to settle for something less than best, but arguably still adequate, in order to reduce cost. In Figure 7.1, the ultimate decision-maker is the base-level asset manager (sub-business unit leader) and the engineering arguments may end up being discounted too readily. However, in Figure 7.2, the base-level engineer is answerable to a more senior engineer who may transmit the recommendation for best engineering practice to his or her boss. In this way, the decision is elevated one level up. Figure 7.3 enables further elevation. Evidently, the longer the engineering line of accountability, the greater the likelihood that best practice engineering solutions will be adopted.

There is another important difference. Where the base-level engineer reports to a base-level asset manager, his or her performance agreement is likely to emphasise contribution to the commercial goals of the asset, perhaps at the expense of engineering excellence. On the other hand, where the base-level engineer reports to a more senior engineer, the performance agreement is more likely to emphasise engineering goals.

Chapter

7

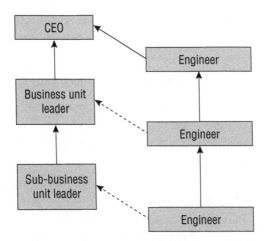

FIGURE 7.3: Engineering line reporting to CEO —
a "centralised" or "functional" organisation

Finally, the longer the engineering line of accountability, the better the career structure for engineers within the organisation and the greater the chances of mentoring and training for engineers.

This discussion has postulated only three decision-making levels but, in any large corporation, there may be half a dozen or more. There is, therefore, a spectrum of possibilities. At one end, any conflicts between commercial and engineering considerations are resolved at the base-level asset. At the other end, differences can be elevated to the CEO, if necessary, for resolution.

The spectrum can be described as one of decentralised versus centralised decision-making. Where differences of opinion are resolved at the base-level asset, without involving higher-level decision-makers, we can speak of decentralised decision-making; where the organisational structure encourages differences to be raised at a higher level, as in Figures 7.2 and 7.3, we can speak of centralised decision-making. While the language of centralisation/decentralisation suggests just two options, this discussion makes it clear that there are degrees of centralisation, and that organisations may position themselves at various points along the spectrum.

Where engineering integrity is paramount, more centralised organisational structures are considered preferable. The contrary point of view is that best practice engineering solutions may be unnecessarily conservative, amounting to "gold-plating" when perhaps "nickel-plating" would do. On this view, the lower-level asset manager is ultimately accountable for his or her decisions and is best placed to balance the competing commercial and engineering imperatives. Moreover, resolving matters at lower levels is more time-efficient. Hence, where commercial considerations are paramount, decentralised organisational structures are considered preferable. Interestingly, companies sometimes cycle between these two organisational designs as their circumstances change.

BP's organisational structure — context and history[1]

At the time of the Macondo accident, BP was among the most decentralised of the major oil and gas companies. It consisted of a series of relatively autonomous regional businesses, only loosely tied together at the corporate centre in London.

At the other extreme stood ExxonMobil, a highly centralised organisation. BHP Billiton Petroleum is another company which appears to have positioned itself at the centralised end of the spectrum. Its 2010 annual review, written after the Macondo accident, places great emphasis on this. Here are two statements from that review (which are highlighted there in extra large font):

> "At BHP Billiton, we're organised for functional excellence ..."

"The depth of our functional expertise, our centralized expert services at our Houston headquarters and our common worldwide standards allow us to operate anywhere in the world safely, efficiently and with speed."

The review makes the same point at several other places. The theme is so strongly stressed that it is hard not to read it as an attempt to distance itself from the decentralised BP model.

Many companies have tried to get the best of both organisational designs by adopting the so-called "matrix model" in which staff are accountable through both functional and asset management hierarchies. In theory, there is an inherent ambiguity about where decision-making authority lies in matrix organisations but, in practice, it seems to work. Admittedly, this form of dual accountability slows decision-making, leading critics to describe it as "clunky". Nevertheless, its advocates argue that it delivers the advantages of both the decentralised and the centralised organisational structures. The paradigm example of this matrix structure is provided by Shell.

While Shell and ExxonMobil have operated with their respective models for decades, BP has not. In the 1980s, BP operated with a matrix structure, much like Shell's. Management consultants under the influence of American business school thinking recommended to Shell in the 1970s and 1980s that it abandon its matrix model in favour of the fully decentralised model, but Shell resisted. It took the view that, while the decentralised model might work well for business corporations engaged in less hazardous activities, it was not appropriate for the oil and gas industry. However, when John Brown became head of BP exploration and production in 1990, he was far more receptive to the advice of the management consultants. He set about dismantling the matrix and replacing it with a streamlined, decentralised structure, with as few staff at head office as possible. The change was a commercial success, but the seeds were sown for both the Texas City and the Macondo disasters.

Decentralisation and the Texas City disaster

The Texas City Refinery had been under relatively centralised control by its owner, Amoco, until 1998, when BP acquired Amoco.[2] By this time, Brown was the CEO of the whole of BP, which meant that he was ultimately responsible for refining, as well as exploration and production. He immediately decentralised control of the new United States assets, including the Texas City Refinery.

Both the Chemical Safety Board and the Baker Panel identified BP's decentralised organisational structure as having contributed to the Texas City disaster six years later.[3] The Baker Panel, in particular, noted that, in BP's decentralised organisational framework:

Chapter

7

"… the refinery plant manager has a tremendous amount of discretion in running the business. Some people at BP refer to this an 'empowerment ethos'. As [CEO] Brown has described, 'we want them to be entrepreneurs, not bureaucrats doing exactly what they are told from above'."

The Baker Panel emphasised its concern by stating it as a formal finding:

"BP's decentralised management system and entrepreneurial culture have delegated substantial discretion to US refinery managers without clearly defining process safety expectations, responsibilities, or accountabilities."

Following the Texas City accident, BP made significant moves towards greater centralisation. In particular, it established a system of engineering authorities throughout the company who reported up "strong dotted" lines to a high-level engineering authority. However, the primary accountability of all of these individuals was to relevant asset managers.[4] This was not centralisation in the sense described above.

The Gulf of Mexico

The organisational structure of BP's deepwater drilling[5] in the Gulf of Mexico went through the cycle of decentralisation/centralisation mentioned above. When BP acquired the Gulf of Mexico assets in about 2000, it inherited a centralised organisational structure. Almost immediately, this structure was completely decentralised and broken up into constituent assets, each with its own engineering resources. This was seen as beneficial from a business point of view, that is, it was expected to reduce costs.

Recentralisation

Following the Baker Panel and the Chemical Safety Board reports in 2007, there was a reconsideration of this structure and the decision was made to recentralise drilling operations, which occurred in mid-2008. There were two exceptions. First, the exploration[6] drilling group (the group that drilled the Macondo well) remained an autonomous entity, to be centralised later. The second exception was that each well team leader was left with a single operations drilling engineer, reporting directly to him. This was a temporary arrangement, apparently designed to reassure well team leaders about the transition. But it meant that the centralisation was not as clean as it might have been, leading some to describe the new organisation as "hybrid functional". The new structure for all drilling other than exploration drilling is depicted in Figure 7.4.[7]

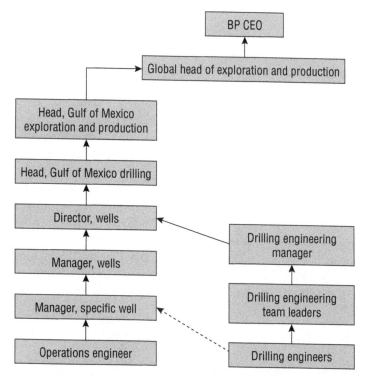

FIGURE 7.4: Organisational structure for drilling engineers, other than exploration drilling, Gulf of Mexico, 2009

As Figure 7.4 makes clear, the new organisation was by no means fully centralised: the drilling engineering manager reported to line managers in the Gulf of Mexico, not to the top of the corporation. This point will be developed shortly.

The aim of the new centralisation was explicitly to improve "engineering excellence". This would have two consequences. First, improving engineering excellence could be expected to improve process safety, as advocated by the Texas City reports. To this extent, the change reflected learning from Texas City. But, second, greater engineering excellence could be expected to improve productivity. BP had formed the view that the other oil and gas majors (particularly ExxonMobil) were more productive precisely because they were more centralised.[8] This productivity argument was, in fact, the most significant driver of the change. Ironically, this was the ultimate repudiation of the business school model. Not only was centralisation safer, it was also more productive!

Exploration drilling

Consider now the case of exploration drilling, which needs to be contrasted with development drilling. Much drilling occurs in areas where hydrocarbon reservoirs have already been discovered, and a number of new wells must be drilled to enable the reserves to be extracted. This is known as development drilling and is relatively straightforward since the geology is already known. Exploration drilling, on the other hand, occurs in new areas where oil and gas is predicted but not yet discovered. This is a more uncertain activity. Exploration drilling is therefore carried out by a specialised group. Typically, BP's exploration group contracted just one rig to do this work, the *Deepwater Horizon*. The decision was made in 2008 not to bring exploration drilling into the new centralised organisational framework and it remained an autonomous group with its own engineering services, as depicted in Figure 7.5. The engineering team leader for this group was thus subordinated to the exploration wells operations manager, not to the drilling engineering manager, who is conspicuously absent from this diagram (compare Figure 7.5 with Figure 7.4). This was a structure that enhanced the flexibility and efficiency of exploration drilling, but at the expense of engineering rigour.

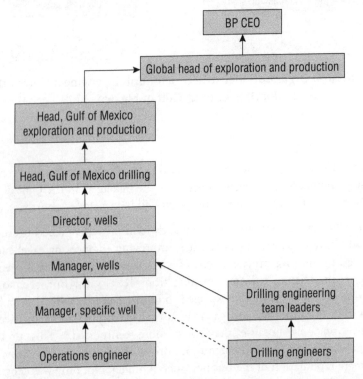

FIGURE 7.5: Organisational structure for exploration drilling, Gulf of Mexico, 2009

The reason that exploration drilling was treated differently is telling.[9] The Vice President (VP) for drilling had wanted to centralise the exploration drilling group, along with the others, but the exploration group resisted. They were on a separate floor in the building in Houston and, for reasons of their own, did not want to be integrated with the others. Moreover, their productivity was good. This meant that the VP did not have a compelling productivity argument for centralising them, as he did with the other groups.

So, in the end, the exploration group remained decentralised *because its productivity was good*. This meant that well integrity issues did not get the same level of scrutiny or higher-level control as was the case for the other drilling groups. Putting it bluntly, safety took a back seat to productivity, although the decision-makers would not have realised this.

Nevertheless, the intention was always to bring exploration drilling into the fold at a later date, and the "go live" date for this turned out to be 14 April 2010, just six days before the accident. The new organisational structure for exploration drilling, as of that date, is depicted in Figure 7.6. The following things should be noted. First, the drilling engineering manager now reported directly to the VP of drilling, one level higher than previously (see Figure 7.4). Second, the change meant that the drilling engineering manager now had authority over the exploration engineers, which, as we shall see, he began to exercise almost straightaway. Third, the exploration engineering team leader now reported up the engineering line, which implicitly enhanced his authority over well team leaders. The significance of this will become apparent shortly. Fourth, an operational drilling engineer continued to report to the Macondo well team leader, rather than to the engineering team leader. This anomalous situation was seen as temporary, to be rectified in the near future.

Chapter

7

The limited centralisation of the engineering function

Even after the centralisation of the Gulf of Mexico organisational structure had been completed in April 2010, BP was still far from a fully centralised organisation. In particular, the engineering function reported into the line several levels below BP's CEO. This situation is starkly evidenced in Figure 7.6. This meant two things. First, the drilling engineering manager for the Gulf of Mexico was subordinated to a Gulf of Mexico asset manager, with all that this entailed. For example, the remuneration of the engineering manager was affected by whether drilling operations in the Gulf of Mexico met their cost reduction targets. Second, it meant that the engineering standards used in the Gulf of Mexico were not necessarily the same as those used in BP operations in other parts of the world. The structure, in others words, allowed for global variation in the standards that BP used. This increased the likelihood that BP's operations in some parts of the world might be, in a sense, "sub-standard".

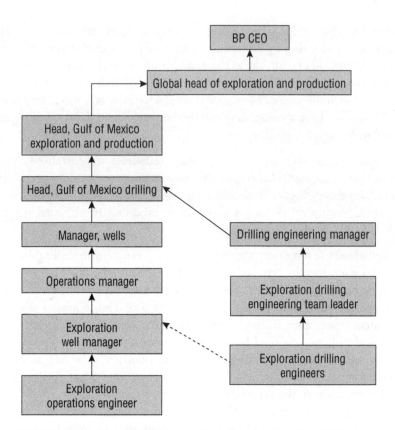

FIGURE 7.6: Organisational structure for exploration drilling, Gulf of Mexico, post-14 April 2010

The impact of the new organisational structure

The decision-making process in the days immediately before the Macondo accident appeared to many of those involved to be quite chaotic. Perhaps in response to this situation, one of the first things that the engineering manager did when he assumed his position of authority over the exploration group was to ask them to develop a decision tree to help with decision-making. The particular purpose was to be sure that everyone understood the conditions under which they would use the cement evaluation tool (the cement bond log). The engineering team leader, who was new in his post but not new to the issues, was also asking hard questions and urging a more cautious approach on certain points. At one stage, he told the Macondo well manager[10] that they needed to "honour the model", which was predicting difficulties with the cement job if they went ahead as planned.[11] The Macondo well manager accepted both of these interventions and, in so doing, recognised that these individuals had some authority with respect to his decisions, even though he was not directly accountable to either.

However, the Macondo well manager resented these interventions. In an email to his operational boss, entitled "The way we work with engineering", he declared that his group "had come to their wits end … this huge level of paranoia from engineering leadership is driving chaos". But what was paranoia to the well manager was no more than good engineering practice to the engineering team leader. Clearly, the new regime was beginning to bite. The well manager's email to his boss went on to make the following enigmatic comment: "This operation is not Thunderhorse." Thunderhorse was a massive state-of-the-art BP rig that nearly capsized as a result of engineering failures. Presumably, the well manager is suggesting that the level of engineering scrutiny that would have been appropriate for Thunderhorse was not appropriate for the Macondo well. At least with hindsight, we can see that he was quite wrong on this point.

There is no doubt that the reorganisation created uncertainty and conflict just days before the incident. This raises the question of whether this uncertainty and conflict may have contributed to the incident. The report of the Chief Counsel for the Oil Spill Commission emphasises the "confusion" and "distraction" that was created by the organisational change,[12] but it does not explicitly claim that this contributed to the accident. The report is disingenuous about this. If there is no causal connection, why mention the issue at all? The less than careful reader of the Chief Counsel's report will draw the inference that there *is* a connection and will assume that this is what the report is intending to convey. The fact is that there is no evidence that confusion engendered by the organisational change contributed to the accident. We have already seen that poor engineering decision-making was a major contributing factor. The interventions by the engineering leadership in the days before the incident were an attempt to improve the quality of this decision-making. Unfortunately, they came too late to have the intended effect. The problem was not confusion; it was that the new ways of thinking and the new modes of decision-making had not taken full effect by the time of the incident.

Summary
In summary, the organisational restructuring on which BP was engaged in the Gulf of Mexico could be expected to generate greater engineering integrity over time. Unfortunately, it occurred in stages, leaving the exploration group as the last to come under more centralised engineering control. This group remained a law unto itself[13] until 14 April and it had not been brought effectively to heel six days later. As a result, a series of flawed engineering decisions were made, leading to the failure of the cement job and, more importantly, the *failure to recognise* that the cement job had failed.

BP's response since the Macondo accident

According to BP's statement to the National Academy of Engineers, the company has made a number of radical organisational changes since the Macondo accident, perhaps the most dramatic being a shift to the ExxonMobil model. It has entirely reorganised its upstream business into three globally operating divisions, Exploration, Development (including drilling) and Production, each with a newly appointed Executive Vice President. These three do not answer to a Chief Executive for Exploration and Production; that post has been abolished. Instead, they answer directly to the CEO of the BP group as a whole.[14] Within Development, BP has created a single Global Wells Organisation which will operate to uniform standards.[15] However, it is not clear in the National Academy of Engineers statement exactly how the engineering function articulates with line management.

As well as this, five months after the accident, BP made the following announcement:[16]

> "BP is to create a new safety division with sweeping powers to oversee and audit the company's operations around the world. The Safety and Operational Risk [S&OR] function will have authority to intervene in all aspects of technical activities. It will have its own expert staff embedded in BP's operating units, including exploration projects and refineries. It will be responsible for ensuring that all operations are carried out to common standards, and for auditing compliance with those standards. The powerful new organisation is designed to strengthen safety and risk management across the BP group. [Its head will report directly to BP's chief executive.]"

In this context, BP is using "operational risk" interchangeably with "process safety risk". The company announced that, at full strength, S&OR would have about 900 people located in both its central organisation and deployed in BP's upstream and downstream businesses.[17] Most importantly, the S&OR people embedded in the various businesses would report to the head of S&OR, not to the relevant business unit leader:[18]

> "Locally deployed personnel report to a VP for S&OR for the relevant business division [as opposed to the business leader]. While the S&OR VPs serve on the leadership teams of their respective [business] divisions, they report to [the head of S&OR] and are therefore independent of the divisional business heads."

The structure of S&OR was thus that of a function, reporting in at the very top of the corporation, but intimately involved in directing the activity of the business units or assets. Its functional structure could be expected to maximise its independence from business pressures and strengthen its capacity to enforce standard practices across the company.

This development built on an initiative taken in 2005 after the Texas City disaster. At that time, BP created a Safety and Operations function at the corporate level. Its head did not, however, report to the CEO. It had an audit function, but the CEO at the time was not committed to giving it the resources that might have made it truly effective. "We have too many people doing checks on the checkers", he said.[19] Nor did it have staff *embedded* in the business units. The new S&OR function is thus a further step in the direction of centralised technical control of the company.

Conclusion

BP radically decentralised its North American operations when it acquired them from Amoco and Arco in 1998 and 2000. From 2005 onwards, it experienced a string of disastrous events — the Texas City Refinery explosion, the collapse of the Thunderhorse platform in the Gulf of Mexico, the oil leak leading to the shutdown of the Prudhoe Bay pipeline in Alaska, and finally, the Macondo blowout. It is hard to escape the conclusion that BP's decentralisation, aimed at maximising profits, is somehow related to this string of disasters. Since the Texas City accident, BP had been slowly recentralising in order to ensure that the engineering function was not subordinated to short-term commercial ends. That slow process of recentralisation was under way in the Gulf of Mexico, but it was too late to prevent the Macondo incident.

Chapter

7

To return, finally, to that incident, the argument here is that, although drilling operations were being slowly centralised in the Gulf of Mexico, the exploration drilling group remained outside the fold, operating autonomously, until too late. Had it been brought in earlier, the quality of engineering decision-making would have improved and the blowout might well have been averted. If one had had to predict in early April 2010 which of BP's Gulf of Mexico drilling teams would experience a disastrous blowout, one might well have predicted the exploration team, not just because exploration drilling is more uncertain than development drilling, but also because this team was under weaker engineering control than was the case for other drilling operations in the Gulf of Mexico.

Endnotes

1 Unless otherwise indicated, this section draws on Bergin, 2011, ch 1.

2 Bergin, 2011, p 35.

3 CSB, 2007, pp 150, 151; Baker et al, 2007, pp 92, 94.

4 See Baker et al, 2007, pp 41, 42. For a more extensive discussion, see Hopkins, 2008, pp 101–103.

5 After a well has been drilled, it is usually plugged and "abandoned" until the time is right to bring the well into production. At that time, the well is "completed", that is, made ready for production and connected to appropriate platforms. The relevant BP nomenclature is therefore "drilling and completions", not "drilling". However, attention here is restricted to the drilling phase and I shall refer to "drilling", not "drilling and completions", in everything that follows.

6 Actually, the "exploration and appraisals" drilling group. For present purposes, appraisal may be regarded as a variation of exploration. For simplicity, I shall refer only to exploration in this book.

7 Figures 7.4, 7.5 and 7.6 are constructed from charts drawn up by the BOEMRE inquiry and from CCR, p 31.

8 Bergin, 2011, pp 116, 117.

9 Personal communication.

10 The well team leader.

11 DWI, 7 October, am, Walz, p 220.

12 CCR, pp 226, 227.

13 For example, it failed to carry out a formal risk assessment of the annulus cement barriers, as required by the technical practice. CCR, p 227; BP, 2010, pp 36, 37.

14 BP, 2011, p 30.

15 BP, 2011, p 46.

16 Statement on BP website, release date 29 September 2010.

17 BP, 2011, p 44.

18 BP, 2011, p 45.

19 Bergin, 2011, p 121.

CHAPTER 8

LEARNING

In *Failure to Learn*, I identified a number of reasons for BP's failure to learn from earlier incidents, among them, its organisational structure and its incentive system. This chapter offers some further thoughts on why learning appears to be so difficult when it comes to high-consequence, low-probability events. It deals with both organisational and individual learning. I am frequently asked how organisations can combat complacency and promote individual learning, and so the chapter concludes with some very specific, practical suggestions.

The type of learning we are talking about here is rather different from the learning advocated by management experts. From their point of view, a learning organisation is one that responds rapidly and flexibly to the business environment, in a process of trial and error learning that maximises commercial success. This is best achieved by a decentralised organisational structure of independent business units. BP had been seen as the epitome of a learning organisation in this respect.[1] Unfortunately, such a structure discourages learning about how to prevent rare but catastrophic events. It is the latter kind of learning that is the subject of this chapter, and readers will need to keep this in mind in what follows.

Organisational learning

It is often claimed that rapid staff turnover erodes corporate memory. On this view, the memory of an organisation is nothing more than the combined memory of its members. A corollary is that organisational learning is reducible to learning by the individual members of the organisation.

But this is not the only or the most useful way to think about organisational learning. An organisation can be said to have learnt from an incident if it changes its structure, procedures, resourcing priorities, or performance indicators, or makes some other organisational change in response to the incident.[2] Assuming that such changes are real and not merely cosmetic, the learning from the incident will be incorporated into the organisation and will survive the departure of any or all of those directly involved in the incident. Admittedly, such changes are made by individuals at the top of the organisation and may be vulnerable when those people move on but, with that proviso, organisational change transcends individuals. In short, organisational learning involves embedding the lessons from an incident in the organisation itself, not in the individuals who make up the organisation. Of course, organisational learning will promote individual learning in various ways, a theme that will be taken up later.

We can go further than this and observe that learning organisations are not simply made up of individuals who learn; they are organisations that have structures and procedures to ensure that lessons from incidents are themselves incorporated as organisational changes. In particular, they have highly developed reporting procedures and they devote resources to analysing reports, and identifying and implementing lessons learnt.* All too often, organisations aspire to be learning organisations without realising these resource implications.[3]

This analysis makes it clear that organisational learning from incidents depends on individual learning by people at the top of the organisation. It is only when they can personally see the need for changes to structure, resources, and so on, that those changes will be made. Perhaps this is why large organisations find it so difficult to learn from incidents. It is only when those incidents have an impact on top decision-makers that we can expect an organisational response.

Did BP learn from Texas City?

Given that the Macondo incident was BP's second catastrophic incident in five years, let us start by asking what BP as an organisation learnt from the first incident — the Texas City Refinery disaster of 2005, in which 15 people died. It didn't learn as much as it needed to, and it has learnt a great deal more from the Macondo incident, but it certainly did learn from Texas City.

The most widely assimilated lessons from the Texas City incident were also the most tangible. One of these was the need to keep people out of harm's way as much as possible. This meant minimising the number of people working close to potential explosion sources and providing blast-proof walls to protect those who could not be moved away. The other tangible outcome concerned the use of open vents that had the potential to release heavier than air hydrocarbons. These were all replaced with flares that would ignite escaping material at the point of release, so preventing a build-up of flammable gas at ground level, as had occurred at Texas City. These changes were driven from the top of the BP hierarchy.

---

* I am referring here to the whole literature on high reliability organisations (see, in particular, Weick & Sutcliffe, 2007), as well as the literature on safety culture (see, in particular, Reason, 1997, ch 10). Here is a practical example: HAZOP teams often approach their task by identifying plausible scenarios and ruling out others on the grounds that they are not "credible". The reality is that these non-credible events may already have occurred either at the plant being HAZOPed or ones like it. Good HAZOP teams will therefore seek to assemble relevant incident histories before they begin. In this way, they learn from past incidents.

However, BP did not make the big organisational changes it needed to make. It left largely intact the decentralised organisational structure which had enabled parts of BP, and Texas City in particular, to operate a long way short of best practice — indeed, to adopt a culture of "casual compliance", as it was called at Texas City. There were some gestures towards strengthening the central engineering function after the Texas City accident, but these did not impact on engineering decision-making at Macondo. It was only after the Macondo incident that BP radically centralised its exploration and production operations (as described in Chapter 7) in such a way as to give a high priority to engineering excellence.

Nor, following Texas City, did BP make radical changes to its bonus arrangements that provided greater rewards for production than for safety. Only after the Macondo incident did this issue finally come to the fore. The new CEO said in October 2010:[4]

> "We are conducting a fundamental review of how we incentivise and reward performance, with the aim of encouraging excellence in safety and risk management. I am a great believer that you get the behaviours that you incentivise. To make it clear that this is our absolute priority, in the current quarter we have made performance in safety, compliance and operational risk management the sole criterion for performance reward across our operating businesses."

The results of the longer-term review have not been made public.

Macondo came close to destroying BP financially, in a way that Texas City did not, and it is hard to escape the conclusion that it was this that forced the top echelons to make the changes which they had failed to make after Texas City.

Failure to learn from blowout-related incidents

Although BP did learn some of the lessons from Texas City, it does not seem to have developed the capacity to learn effectively from other incidents.

Eighteen months before the Macondo blowout, BP suffered a blowout in the Caspian Sea. Fortunately, there was no ignition, but 211 people were evacuated from a production platform. The field was shut in for months, causing major production losses. The blowout was apparently the result of a poor cement job.[5] This is the kind of event that provides an ideal learning opportunity. It was very big, very disturbing and very costly, and it impacted significantly on BP's partners in the Caspian Sea venture — Chevron, ExxonMobil and others. The lesson was that BP needed to pay much more attention to ensuring good cement jobs. But this lesson was not assimilated by BP engineers far away in the Gulf of Mexico. If it had been, they could not have taken as cavalier an attitude to the Macondo cement job as they did.*

There was a second learning opportunity much closer to home from which BP failed to benefit. On 8 March 2010, a little over a month before the blowout, the Macondo well experienced a significant kick. It took the rig crew 33 minutes to realise that the well was flowing, which could only mean that they were not monitoring the well as they were required to.[6] The team later admitted that they had "screwed up",[7] and BP required Halliburton to remove one of the individuals responsible for the poor monitoring.[8] A "lessons learnt" document was distributed within the BP Gulf of Mexico drilling organisation.[9] But BP did not enter this incident in its incident reporting system and did not carry out the kind of investigation required by its own policies.[10]

Essentially the same team involved in the monitoring failure on 8 March was responsible for the monitoring failure that preceded the blowout on 20 April. Admittedly, the circumstances were different: on the second occasion, the team believed that the well had been successfully cemented and it was this that led them to drop their guard. But drop their guard they did. Whatever learning there had been from the 8 March incident had been minimal, and BP had not taken effective steps to ensure that the lessons from that incident were embedded in the organisation.

A third failure to learn is particularly relevant to the Macondo event. This failure was primarily Transocean's, not BP's. On 23 December 2009, just four months before the Macondo blowout, Transocean experienced a remarkably similar event in United Kingdom waters while completing a well for Shell. On this occasion, rig staff were displacing the mud in the riser with seawater, just as they were at Macondo. They had previously carried out a reduced pressure test on the well which they declared a success, just as happened at Macondo. They then apparently stopped monitoring and were caught by surprise when mud overflowed onto the rig floor. Fortunately, they were able to shut in the well before an uncontrolled blowout or fire occurred.[11]

After this incident, Transocean created a PowerPoint presentation warning that "tested barriers can fail" and noting that the "risk perception of barrier failure was blinkered" by the reduced pressure test. It concluded that high vigilance is necessary when operating underbalanced with one barrier — exactly the situation

---

* The Montara blowout that occurred off the Australian coast just eight months prior to the Macondo blowout also involved a cement failure and, worse, a failure to recognise that it had failed (Hayes, 2012a). This was a high-profile blowout that had many people in the United States asking: could this happen in the Gulf of Mexico? However, the Montara report appeared after the Macondo blowout and was therefore not available to the Macondo engineers. Whether they would have read it, had it been available, is another matter.

at Macondo. Transocean eventually issued another operations advisory to its North Sea fleet on 14 April, six days before the Macondo incident. Among other things, the advisory admonished:[12]

> "Do not be complacent because the reservoir has been isolated and tested. Remain focused on well control and good well control procedures."

Apparently, neither the PowerPoint presentation nor the advisory had been sent to the *Deepwater Horizon*. Indeed, a Transocean executive with responsibility for the *Deepwater Horizon* was not even aware of the North Sea incident until some time after the Macondo accident.[13] So it was that Transocean in the Gulf of Mexico learnt nothing at all from the North Sea incident.

Explaining these failures to learn

I want to use these examples to explore a little further some of the reasons for the failure to learn. BP's decentralised structure clearly played a part in the failure of BP in the Gulf of Mexico to learn from what happened to BP in the Caspian Sea. Similarly, Transocean's decentralised or divisional structure meant that the lessons from the North Sea never arrived in the Gulf of Mexico. But, even if these lessons had been disseminated in the Gulf of Mexico, there is no guarantee that they would have made a difference; the failure of the *Deepwater Horizon* crew to learn from its own incident is demonstration enough of that.

The learning strategy that many organisations adopt following an incident is to prepare a "lessons learnt" document or an "alert" or "advisory", and to distribute this via email to other parts of the organisation. They then bemoan the fact that these documents are not read or implemented. The problem is that, for a message to be successfully communicated, it must be both transmitted and received. Many large organisations devote the necessary resources to ensuring that the message is transmitted, but they do not devote comparable resources to ensuring that it is received. The arrival of an email in an inbox does not guarantee that real communication will occur. There needs to be a resource at the receiving end, comparable in some way to the resource at the transmitting end, dedicated to receiving incoming "lessons learnt" and converting them into actions. Those actions themselves may involve additional resources. For example, if lessons about the importance of monitoring wells at all stages of drilling operations are to be properly learnt, it may be necessary to set up a program to audit compliance. Or it may be that mudloggers should be required to report regularly on whether there have been any impediments to monitoring, as there were in the final hours before the Macondo blowout. To merely admonish people to be more vigilant, as the Transocean advisory did, is predictably futile.

Individual learning

Transocean's strategy of warning that tested barriers can fail, and highlighting the need for vigilance, is clearly aimed at educating individuals, not at encouraging organisational changes. It seeks individual learning, not organisational learning. There are some very fundamental reasons why individual learning is problematic as a strategy for preventing rare but catastrophic events. These must be understood if learning by individuals is to be made more effective.

Let us begin with a distinction between what I shall call experience-based learning and theoretical learning. This is roughly the distinction that psychologists make between behaviourist learning and cognitive learning,[14] but I shall use "experience-based" and "theoretical" in the hope that these are more readily intelligible terms.

Experience-based learning relies on feedback from our own experience.[15] If we do something that delivers a benefit, with no negative consequences, the behaviour is positively reinforced. If there are negative consequences, we are less likely to do it again. For example, if I take a short cut and it works, I am likely to do it again and it quickly becomes the norm. This was described in Chapter 3 as the "normalisation of deviation". If it doesn't work, I learn not to do it again. This is trial and error learning. It is arguably the most basic and most powerful form of human learning.

The other form of learning, theoretical learning, involves seeking out new information, problem solving and remembering. It involves learning from the experience of others, not just oneself. According to the Latin proverb, "a wise man learns by the mistakes of others, a fool by his own". The proverb is unfairly dismissive of the role of experience-based learning, but it does highlight the fact that theoretical learning may be more difficult.

Not surprisingly, for practical men and women on the job (drillers, for example), the predominant form of learning is experience-based. Here is how one researcher has tried to capture the learning strategy of drillers:[16]

> "The drillers' mindset is shaped by the years of experience and on the job training required to achieve their role ... Drillers are at once resistant to new methods of training, and open to anything that works. It's more an inductive, heuristic perspective rather than analytical and deductive."

In this context, "inductive" means drawing conclusions on the basis of past experience, while "deductive" corresponds to theoretical learning.

The problem is that, when it comes to rare but catastrophic events, these modes of learning may be in conflict. Defence-in-depth requires multiple independent defences. The theory tells us that, if one of the barriers is routinely bypassed, the risk of disaster increases. Worse, if different people bypass different defences without each other's knowledge, the effectiveness of the system of defence-in-depth may rapidly erode without anyone realising. This is what led to the tragic shooting down of two United Nations helicopters by US jets in Iraq in 1994.[17] Or, again, if the barriers are not in fact independent, bypassing one may effectively undermine others, as happened in the Macondo case. These things we know from the study of other events. It is theoretical knowledge. On the other hand, personal experience may tell us that a particular defence can be routinely ignored without consequence. That seems to have been the case for the drillers who were preparing for departure after the Macondo well had been cemented and tested. Their experience-based learning contributed to the disaster.

This analysis helps to illuminate the idea of "complacency". Recall Transocean's response to the North Sea blowout — "do not be complacent", its advisory said. Similarly, the inquiry by the regulator concluded that "overall complacency of the *Deepwater Horizon* crew was a possible contributing cause of the kick detection failure" and hence of the blowout.[18]

Complacency, however, is a moral failing, a bit like carelessness. And singling out moral failure as a contributing factor does little to advance the cause of accident prevention. The reality is that people learn that so-called complacent behaviour works. Complacency is the product of practical experience which, as we know, is considerably more influential than abstract knowledge about risk. It is obvious, therefore, that railing against complacency, as the Transocean advisory did, is unlikely to have the intended effect.

Harnessing experience-based learning

It is, however, possible to harness experience-based learning, even in relation to rare but catastrophic events. Consider, first, the problem of "complacency". Even though there may normally be no catastrophic consequences from taking shortcuts or bypassing a defence, an organisation can *create* consequences. If it puts in place supervisory and auditing procedures that identify non-compliance, and if it imposes consequences when non-compliance is detected, then, assuming that these consequences follow with some degree of certainty, people will quickly learn to comply. Far too often organisations impose consequences for non-compliance only when there has been an incident. That is not what is being suggested here. The whole point is that there may never be a disastrous incident. The consequences must follow from the non-compliance itself. I am not suggesting that organisations expand the list of rules for which people can be dismissed. People learn from much less draconian consequences, provided those consequences are consistent and reasonably certain — this is a basic finding of criminological research. The point is simply illustrated: being caught for speeding once or twice tends to slow most people down.

A second way to draw on experienced-based learning in the context of rare but catastrophic events is to train people on simulators, where they can experience abnormal conditions and learn by trial and error how to deal with them. Aircraft cockpit simulators are now so good that pilots who are trained on them can transfer directly to scheduled flights with paying passengers, without the need for any additional training on real aircraft. Similarly, control room simulators in process industries can give operators personal experience of rare events, enabling them to learn by trial and error without blowing up a real plant in the process. BP promised to introduce simulator training for operators at the Texas City Refinery following the 2005 disaster. Unfortunately, five years later, it still had not done so.

Finally, we should note that near misses can also be a source of experience-based learning. Research on the way in which experienced professionals make decisions in high reliability organisations shows that they frequently draw on their own experience of frightening near misses in ways that reinforce their commitment to the system of defence-in-depth. Consider an operations manager at a nuclear power station, whom Jan Hayes interviewed in her research.[19] He had been working on shift in a more junior capacity many years earlier when the power station experienced a significant incident. He still remembered details of that shift, such as the date and day of the week. He said:

> "I think you've got to go through some experience like that ... shall we say you've been blooded then and you realise that sometimes decisions you make thereafter, what implications can come from those decisions or not taking decisions."

This was a man whose personal experience had taught him an important lesson about the prevention of rare but catastrophic events.

Strengthening theoretical learning

Notwithstanding the previous comments, there are limited opportunities for experienced-based learning in relation to rare but catastrophic events. For most people, the available learning strategies are more theoretical, such as drawing on the experience of others. We need, therefore, to think about ways in which such theoretical learning can be strengthened.

A first point to make is that people learn more easily from stories than they do from abstract information or slogans (such as "safety is good for business"). Hence, the most effective learning comes from telling stories about incidents that have happened both inside and outside an organisation.

Storytelling is a natural form of learning that can occur almost spontaneously. Hayes found that the operational managers she interviewed loved sharing stories about their experiences. She argues that this was an important part of their continuing professional development.[20]

Second, simply providing information, even in story form, is not the most effective way to ensure learning. As Lardner reminds us, theoretical learning can be passive or active. "Passive [learning] ... such as listening to a briefing about an incident that happened to someone else, will have limited impact."[21] "Lessons learnt" are sometimes communicated at tool box meetings in this way and predictably have little effect. Learning is best achieved by *doing*. For example, in a university context, people learn by writing essays, doing assignments, carrying out experiments, and so on. Attending lectures is a relatively inefficient way of learning. My own experience is that it is only when I have to lecture on a subject that I truly master it.

Recent research has shown that active or engaged strategies are very much more effective than more passive strategies, *in particular when it comes to learning about major hazards*. It seems that, in this context, active learning methods stimulate a sense of dread that in turn makes the learning more effective.[22]

Putting these points together, one way to enhance theoretical learning, or learning from the experience of others, is to ask people to study some accident and to make a presentation about it — to tell the story — perhaps to their immediate subordinates, perhaps to their peers or even to their superiors. To have to make a presentation to others forces the presenter to engage with the material in a way that few other learning strategies do. It must be emphasised that the benefit of the presentation will primarily be to the presenter, not to the audience, but, if everyone gets a turn at presenting, everyone benefits. These exercises should be conducted as far down the organisational hierarchy as possible. Presenters could be asked to choose an external incident of general relevance for the organisation — there are numerous major accident reports that could be used — or they might talk about an external incident that is related to their own area of work. So, a rotating equipment engineer might select an accident involving rotating equipment etc.* People might also give talks on accidents or incidents that have occurred within their own organisation where detailed reports are available. These reports often contain important lessons that are rapidly forgotten unless they are regularly revisited.

Such a learning exercise can be enhanced if, after the presentation, audience members have a discussion about whether or not a similar accident could occur in their context and what the controls are to ensure that it does not.

Chapter

8

---

* A good source for this more specific type of presentation would be the book by Trevor Kletz, *Learning from accidents*, which consists of a series of easily understood case studies (Kletz, 2001).

It is vital that these kinds of presentations be given by people at the top of the organisation, as well as further down. Senior managers sometimes have built into their performance agreements a requirement to attend a certain number of safety events each year. This is unlikely to be an effective learning process if they attend merely as audience members, for the reasons given above. Sometimes their attendance will take the form of giving a presentation on the importance of safety. This often amounts to preaching to the converted and is unlikely to be a learning experience, either for the audience or for the presenter. But, if they make a presentation about the lessons that they have derived from an incident that has occurred either within or without their organisation, the preparation required to make such a presentation will almost certainly be a learning experience. With luck, the audience may also benefit.

One organisation to which I gave this advice responded in an innovative way. It set up a series of "lunch and learn" seminars on process safety. The series began with a presentation on a particular incident, Piper Alpha, but subsequent speakers were asked to make presentations on the significance of process safety in their own context. Here are some of the titles and presenters:

- "What process safety means to non-technical disciplines", presented by the VP for Finance and Head of Legal;
- "What do technical folks do about process safety?", presented by the VP for Production;
- "How do we apply process safety to well design and drilling", presented by an asset manager; and
- "Leadership behaviours — creating a culture of 'chronic unease'", presented by the VP for Commercial.

These will be significant learning experiences for the presenters. The VP for Finance and Head of Legal will almost certainly be out of their comfort zone talking about what process safety means to them, especially if they apply their mind to what they can do to improve process safety. Similarly, the VP for Commercial may never previously have been required to think about and explain the significance of "chronic unease".[23] Even for production managers, to have to articulate the significance of process safety in this way will probably require a good deal of thought. In short, this lunch and learn series is a remarkable effort to ensure that people at the highest level are learning about what it takes to avoid rare but catastrophic events.

In another organisation that I have worked with, an inspirational leader had developed some interesting strategies for learning from incidents. Her organisation had had a practice of sending out bulletins and notifications about incidents, with little apparent effect. Accordingly, she had organised a "process safety book club" and had chosen easy-to-read books on process safety accidents. She held regular video-conferenced discussions on various chapters, followed up by quizzes. In this way, she turned what might otherwise have been a passive learning activity into a far more active experience. Membership of the club was voluntary, but there were hundreds of participants, including some very senior executive managers. She was seeking to create a "culture of reading" about process safety, she said. The book club was part of a broader process safety campaign, the theme of which was "preventing incidents through learning from others".

A final example concerns a CEO who had written into the performance agreement of his subordinates a requirement that they read a particular book about a process safety accident and discuss it with their direct reports.

Conclusion

I was doing observations in an air traffic control room in Australia some years ago when a controller made a mistake that reminded managers of a disastrous mid-air collision over Europe five years earlier. The mistake by the Australian air traffic controller had no consequences and no aircraft was ever in danger. But the story of the mid-air collision in Europe was well known to the Australian managers and they were greatly disturbed that a precursor to such an event had occurred at their own air traffic control centre.[24] Accordingly, they took immediate corrective action.

If the story of the Caspian Sea blowout had been similarly well known to the Macondo engineers, or if the Transocean blowout in UK waters had become part of the common store of knowledge of the *Deepwater Horizon* drillers, it is less likely that they would have made the decisions that led to the Macondo blowout.

Chapter

8

But individuals will only learn the lessons of previous incidents if the organisations that they belong to understand the need for such individual learning and create the conditions under which the learning can occur. It is organisations that need to foster the kinds of storytelling from which everyone can learn. This requires an organisational commitment which, in turn, requires a commitment from the people at the top. It is they who must ensure that the organisations they lead are learning organisations and that the people for whom they are responsible are aware of relevant lessons from previous incidents.

Endnotes

1   Bergin, 2011, p 33.

2   Argoteand and Todrova (2007) define organisational learning as "a change in the organisation which occurs as a function of experience".

3   See Hopkins, 2008, pp 146, 147.

4   Speech to US marketers, 25 October 2010.

5   *Financial Times*, 15 December 2010.

6   BP, 2010, p 107.

7   BOEMRE, p 76.

8   BP, 2011, p 9.

9   BP, 2010, p 107.

10 BOEMRE, p 76.

11 Most of the information on this incident and the response to it comes from the Presidential Commission report (OSC, p 124).

12 DWI, 9 December, pm, Caducci, p 99.

13 DWI, 24 August, Winslow, p 122.

14 Lefrancois, 1994, chs 4 and 5. R Lardner and I Robertson make a similar distinction between direct and indirect learning. The former is based on personal experience; the latter is based on the experience of others. See their paper "Towards a deeper level of learning from incidents: use of scenarios", presented at Hazards XXII, Manchester, 2011.

15 For this reason, I considered using the term "experiential learning". However, there is a literature that distinguishes experiential learning from behaviourist learning so, to avoid confusion, I use the term "experience-based".

16 See P Donley, "This is not about mystics: or why a little science would help a lot", working paper for the Deepwater Horizon Study Group, p 18.

17 Snook, 2000.

18 BOEMRE, pp 110, 111.

19 Jan Hayes, "Operational decision making in high hazard organisations", PhD thesis, Australian National University, September 2009, p 231.

20 Hayes, ibid, p 252.

21 Lardner and Robertson, op cit.

22 Burk et al, 2011.

23 Reason, 1997, pp 37, 214.

24 A fuller account of this incident is given in Hopkins (ed), 2009, pp 25–27.

CHAPTER 9

MANAGEMENT WALK-AROUNDS

About seven hours before the Macondo blowout, four company VIPs were helicoptered onto the *Deepwater Horizon*. They had come on a "management visibility tour" and were actively touring the rig when disaster struck. All four survived.

As we have seen in earlier chapters, there were several indications in the hours before the blowout that the well was not sealed. The touring VIPs, two from BP and two from the rig owner, Transocean, had all worked as drilling engineers or rig managers in the past and had detailed knowledge of drilling operations. Had they focused their attention on what was happening with the well, they would almost certainly have realised the need to intervene. But their attention was focused elsewhere, and an opportunity to avert disaster was lost. This comment is made with hindsight and I am not suggesting that these men were in any way culpable. But there are clearly lessons here for all senior managers who undertake management visibility tours in major hazard facilities.

There is a tragic irony here. A major purpose of the visit was to emphasise the importance of safety, and yet the visitors paid almost no attention to the safety critical activities that were occurring during their visit. What were they doing? Where was their attention focused? How might their visit have had a happier outcome? This chapter offers some answers to these questions. But, first, let us think a little more generally about the purposes of management "walk-arounds", as they are often called.

The purposes of management walk-arounds

Many companies understand that good management requires senior managers to spend time with frontline workers. Some companies build into performance agreements for senior managers a requirement that they conduct a certain number of such site visits each year. Management walk-arounds are regarded by some commentators as "the single most important safety activity an organisation can perform".[1] Among their purposes are the following:

- visibility — to show that management cares;
- to elicit the concerns of staff; and
- to engage in informal safety auditing.

It is sometimes suggested that these purposes are incompatible and cannot be achieved simultaneously. According to King, any attempt to engage in ad hoc auditing will undermine the ability to elicit staff concerns.[2] Moreover, one company that I have visited provides its executives with a prompt card that says: "The purpose is visibility and clear demonstration of interest — NOT inspection."

I note these observations at this point simply to emphasise that these are distinct and contrasting purposes. Whether they are actually inconsistent is something I shall come back to later.

The purposes of the visit to the Deepwater Horizon

BP/Transocean management visibility tours of Gulf of Mexico rigs were regularly scheduled events, and it was more or less by chance that the *Deepwater Horizon* had been selected on this occasion.

The most general purpose of the tour, as the name suggests, was to make management visible to the workforce by meeting and talking with workers on a variety of topics. It was first and foremost a social visit, without a tightly specified agenda. This was the first of the purposes specified above. This aspect of the tour was best exemplified by the group's visit to the bridge to talk to the marine crew. As one of the group explained, the marine crew was often omitted on management visibility tours and they wanted to give "credit" to this group.[3] Another explained that:[4]

> "[The bridge] is kind of an impressive place if you haven't been there. Lots of screens, lots of technology. We had a long visit, a nice visit there. And we also had the chance to work with a dynamic positioning simulator that they have up there used for training and demonstration purposes."

But, in addition to this social function, the visit had a variety of more specific safety-related purposes. The rig had amassed a total of seven years without a lost-time injury and the VIPs wished to congratulate the crew on this achievement and to identify any lessons that might be transferred to other vessels in the fleet.[5] In addition, one of the VIPs was aware of a slip hazard that had been identified on another rig, and he wanted to see if the *Deepwater Horizon* was aware of this hazard and had made appropriate modifications, for example, by installing non-slip materials.[6] The group, in short, was actively engaged in transferring safety lessons from one rig to another.

One of the VIPs had a particular interest in harnesses used for work at heights:[7]

> "One of the things I look for in addition to housekeeping, I look at harnesses and look at when inspections were done on harnesses. And I noticed when I looked into the harness locker some of the harnesses did not have tagging on the inspection tags."

He took this up with the rig manager and received a satisfactory answer. Apart from this, he was interested in asking questions of various employees to check on their understanding of safety culture.[8]

Transocean and BP were, at the time, running a concerted campaign to increase awareness of the risk of hand injury and the risk posed by objects dropped from height. Members of the VIP group spoke about this campaign on several occasions to different crew members. This was the most consistently stressed theme of the visit.

It is clear from this account that this was a lot more than just a social visit or a management visibility tour. These visitors were very much focused on safety. They came with messages about safety and each in his own way was engaged in an informal safety auditing process. Referring back to the purposes mentioned in the previous section, they saw no incompatibility between this auditing activity on the one hand and showing concern and interest on the other.

The failure of the VIPs to discover what was going on

Given that the visitors were engaged in a variety of informal auditing and fact-finding activities, let us consider how close they came to discovering that the warnings of a blowout were being systematically missed or misinterpreted.

Soon after their arrival, the VIPs visited the drilling shack, the centre of drilling operations. They found the rig personnel engaged in discussion about how to do the well integrity test. The BP man on the rig told one of the visiting BP executives: "We're having a little trouble getting lined up [for the test] but it's no big deal."[9] There was far more to it than this, as we saw in Chapter 3, and the crew had in fact got it horribly wrong. But the BP executive asked no more questions and moved on to a social conversation about the history of the company — "ARCO days and Alaska days".

Presumably, because the rig was owned by Transocean, the senior Transocean executive in the VIP party assumed the de facto role of tour host. He noted that the tone of the conversation he heard among the drillers was confused.[10] He sensed that they needed help — a sixth sense that drillers have, he said.[11] As a result of this intuition, he suggested that the on-site rig manager, who was accompanying the

VIPs on their tour, should stay behind to help,[12] and that the VIPs should move on so as not to distract the people engaged in the reduced pressure test.

Later in the day, he asked the on-site rig manager if the test had gone well and was given the thumbs up.[13] His question clearly invited the response he got. It was more a conversational question than a serious inquiry. He did not probe for evidence and simply accepted the reassurance he was given.

The VIPs said later that they would have been available to provide advice, had they been asked, but they were not asked and so did not concern themselves further with what was going on. There was no recognition that this was an opportunity to do some auditing, to check on the competence of the people involved, and to verify that they were complying with procedures that were critical to the safety of the well and the rig.

In retrospect, this was a tragedy. Something was going seriously wrong before their eyes but, because of the constraints they had imposed on themselves (to be discussed below), they turned away and investigated no further. Not only was an opportunity lost to do some informal auditing, but so too was an opportunity lost to avoid disaster.

Apart from the reduced pressure test, there was a second missed opportunity to avoid disaster later that afternoon. The drillers were in the process of substituting seawater for the drilling mud in the riser (the column between the rig and the sea floor). As described in Chapter 4, the rig crew should have been monitoring the volume coming out of the riser to ensure that it matched what was going in. In fact, they weren't. For long periods, the outflow was being sent directly overboard, first to a supply vessel and later into the sea, in both cases bypassing the rig's most important outflow monitoring systems.

Had any of the VIPs asked the question that afternoon, "how are you monitoring flows?", they would certainly have realised that no effective monitoring was taking place. Had they then intervened to ensure effective monitoring, the disaster would not have happened. The VIP team understood that the rig was in the process of removing one of the last safeguards against blowout (the mud in the riser), but they did not inquire as to what was happening and did not see this as an opportunity to audit how the safety of the well was being managed.

There was good reason to expect that the VIP team would have paid more attention to the mud replacement process than they did. As we saw in Chapter 8, Transocean had suffered a near disastrous blowout in the North Sea, off the coast of Scotland, four months earlier.[14] The circumstances were very similar. Workers had tested the well and were replacing mud with seawater. Because the well had passed the test, they were not paying attention to flows in and out. But the crew had let its guard down prematurely. The well was not secure and a blowout ensued.

Given that members of the VIP group were intent on checking that the *Deepwater Horizon* rig had learned from earlier incidents in the fleet, it would have been appropriate to check whether the crew had learned the lessons from the blowout in the North Sea. However, the VIPs were unaware of the North Sea event[15] and there was no attempt to ensure that this critical lesson had been learnt.

Explaining the behaviour of the VIPs

The preceding discussion identifies some surprising gaps in the activities of the VIPs. How are we to make sense of this? How can we account for their failure to take advantage of the important auditing opportunities available to them that day?

Behaviours and conditions

There are several things at work here. I begin by making a distinction between behaviours (actions, decisions) on the one hand, and conditions or relatively unchanging states on the other. The VIPs appeared to focus their informal auditing activities on checking that certain conditions were as they should be, rather than checking on behaviours. So, for example, they checked on whether the harness tests were up to date, whether a certain slip hazard had been remedied, and whether housekeeping was up to standard. They did not set out to check on what people were actually doing at the time and whether they were complying with safety requirements. This is a common auditing preference. States or conditions are easier to audit because they are relatively unchanging. They await the arrival of the auditor and can be assessed at a time of the auditor's choosing. On the other hand, compliance with procedures, especially where the behaviour is intermittent, is much harder to audit. The auditor needs to catch the behaviour at the time it is occurring. If the auditor does not make a special effort to be present at relevant times, the behaviour will be missed. This is why behaviour on night shifts is notoriously less compliant than on day shifts. Given that the VIPs were touring according to their own schedule, it was far easier for them to plan to audit conditions than behaviours.

There is a second reason why the VIPs preferred to audit conditions. They were concerned not to interfere in what was going on — they did not want to disrupt activities. The decision to limit their time on the floor of the drilling rig was explicitly motivated by this concern. They were also aware that, because of their seniority, any interventions on their part had the potential to undermine the authority of the managers on board the rig. Their policy, therefore, was to audit as unobtrusively as possible, which on the whole meant not examining too closely what people were actually doing.

Chapter

9

A third reason for not inquiring too closely about what people were actually doing was provided by another BP executive who testified at one of the inquiries but who was not present on the VIP tour. "You are managing a group of professionals who have very clear responsibilities",[16] he said. The implication here is that to question what they are doing is to doubt their professionalism, which this man was clearly unwilling to do. He was asked:[17]

> "How would you ensure that people [who are] answering to you are actually doing their job if you're not doing spot checks or having some type of accountability to make sure they're doing what you're paying them to do?"

He answered:

> "We would check with people what they're doing but this would go down through the chain of command. So you know, I wouldn't necessarily go direct to a single person, I may go to his manager [and ask:] Are we on track? Are things going OK? Are we managing the way we should be?"

There are two problems with this approach. First, the questions suggested in the previous quote are so subtle that the manager may not even pick up that he is being questioned about the competence of his subordinates. The other problem is that, if the manager himself is less than competent in some respect, he will be unaware of any similar deficiencies in those he manages. This appears to have been part of the problem on the *Deepwater Horizon*. Be that as it may, there is an obvious reluctance here to test competency by engaging directly with the people concerned. This attitude was almost certainly present in the minds of the VIPs touring the rig, which meant in particular that the lack of competence of those engaged in the pressure testing went unrecognised. President Obama said after the oil spill that henceforth government agencies would need to "trust but verify" that oil companies were doing the right thing. Perhaps senior executives need to apply the same philosophy to their subordinate managers.

There is at least one qualification that needs to be made to the preceding observations about non-intervention. One of the VIPs did say: "… if we happen upon someone who appears to be doing something extremely critical [read 'dangerous'], we might take the opportunity to have a conversation with them. But otherwise we don't cross any barrier tapes and we don't interfere."[18] In other words, if something stands out from a distance as dangerous, he would take some action. An example might be seeing someone working at height without a harness. But, as this man suggests, this is an exception to the general, self-imposed rule.

Major hazard risk

Another quite distinct factor contributed to the failure of the VIPs to focus on what was going on that afternoon. To understand how this operated, we must first recall the distinction between occupational or personal safety on the one hand, and process safety on the other. In Chapter 5, we saw how, for BP, safety meant occupational safety. This was a matter of policy. The safety in "HSE" was explicitly restricted to occupational safety, and process safety slipped into the background. The situation was much the same for Transocean.

This was the general mindset that the VIPs took with them to the rig. Their informal safety auditing activity was focused on occupational safety, not process safety. Hence, they were highly focused on things that might cause injury to an individual — a slip hazard, a faulty harness, and housekeeping not up to scratch. They were not at all focused on how major hazard risk was being managed (for example, the adequacy of the pressure testing) or whether people were following appropriate well control procedures (such as monitoring mud flows). These matters lay outside the scope of their informal auditing activities. Perhaps one of the clearest illustrations was a conversation that the VIPs had with the individual who was transferring mud to the supply boat. They discussed how he might minimise the risks to himself when doing this job, but they did not query the appropriateness of what he was doing or ask how the outflow was being monitored.

This one-sided concentration on occupational or personal safety has been identified as a contributor to many previous process safety accidents, including the BP Texas City Refinery disaster of 2005. It remains an issue for BP and was one of the underlying reasons for the failure of the VIPs on that fateful afternoon to recognise that the rig was on a path to disaster.

Summary

The informal auditing activities of the VIPs on the *Deepwater Horizon* were limited in two ways. First, they tended to focus on conditions rather than behaviour, partly in order to avoid disrupting ongoing activities. This meant that the VIPs avoided looking in detail at the behaviour of the people who were engaged in well operations that afternoon. Second, the focus of safety for these VIPs, and for their companies, was on managing conventional safety hazards, not major process safety hazards. Again, this diverted the group's attention from the operations that were underway. Had the VIP group not been limited in these ways, it is possible that they would have identified some of the mistakes and non-compliances that were occurring at the time of their visit and intervened in such a way as to prevent the accident.

Chapter

9

Stopping the job

Before moving on, let us reflect a little further on the concern shown by the VIPs not to disrupt ongoing activities. One of the behaviours that BP and Transocean were trying to instil in their workers was that they could and should stop the job when something was amiss. People who stopped the job for safety reasons were acknowledged and even rewarded,[19] and inquiry witnesses said that stopping the job for safety reasons was relatively common.[20] However, in all cases where the job had been stopped, the issue was a perceived risk to an individual, such as a risk that an object might be dropped on someone. Witnesses were not aware of instances where drilling or other well operations had been stopped for safety reasons. This issue was highlighted by the evidence of one of the mudloggers.[21] He had been "uncomfortable" about the simultaneous operations that were making it difficult for him to monitor mud flows in the hours before the blowout, but it did not occur to him to try to stop the job, even though he knew in general terms about the stop the job policy. He said later that he should have stopped the job.

There are a number of reasons why the stop the job policy does not, in practice, apply to major hazards,* but the point to be made here is that the behaviour of the VIPs unwittingly reinforced the view that the policy did not apply in these circumstances. If the job was too important to be interrupted by VIPs, the subliminal message was that one would need a very good reason indeed to justify stopping the job. In this way, the concern of the VIPs not to disrupt rig activities undermined the stop the job policy in the case of major hazard risks.**

---

* The mudlogger chose not to stop the job, in part because he did not perceive an immediate threat (DWI, 7 December, Keith, p 238). This is perhaps the nub of the problem. The control of major hazard risks depends on the concept of defence-in-depth, which requires that there be multiple barriers or checks in place. The problem is that the failure of any one of these is usually not perceived as increasing the risk significantly. It is therefore hard to argue that the failure of any one barrier is sufficient to stop the operation in its tracks.

** I was once asked by a mining company CEO to take safety culture soundings in several of the company's mines. I was told I could stop mining in order to talk to workers if I wanted to. So, at one mine, I asked that the whole operation be stopped in order to talk to miners at the face. This was resented by the miners themselves, whose bonuses were at stake, so nothing much was gained from this conversation. On arrival back at the surface, I was greeted by the mine manager who first asked what seemed like a ritual question about whether I had identified any issues that required his immediate attention. His duty done, he went on to tell me quite aggressively that the stoppage I had requested had cost $20,000 worth of production. I was shocked. If he was willing to speak in this way to me, a representative of the CEO, it would be a very brave miner who tried to stop production for safety reasons. I am reminded of the work of the sociologist, Harold Garfinkle (1967). He suggested that the best way to understand the rules that are implicitly operating in a social order is experimentally to disrupt them. The manager's reaction to my disruption of his social order demonstrated the power of the production imperative operating at this mine.

Several readers of earlier drafts of this chapter have objected that it would not have been appropriate for a group of visiting VIPs to interrupt a time-critical activity. That may or may not be so. But the people on the *Deepwater Horizon* were not in a time-critical situation. The crew spent more than an hour discussing the anomalies and arguing about the meaning of the various signs. A VIP could easily have joined this group, initially as an observer, without hindering the process. Again, the VIPs who talked to the man who was offloading mud to the supply vessel could easily have asked him about why he was doing what he was doing, without being disruptive. In short, there will be many situations in which executives on walk-arounds can talk to people about what they are doing without disrupting activities.

A more effective executive safety auditing strategy

The limitations of VIP auditing on the *Deepwater Horizon* challenge us to think constructively about how these executives might have gone about their informal safety auditing in a more effective way. Here are some suggestions.

First, prior to the visit, they would have reminded themselves of the major accident events that were possible on the rig. Sometimes, if executives are not experts, they may need to be briefed about this. One of the executives on this tour was indeed provided with a briefing about matters he could discuss. The briefing included such things as the productivity of the rig (non-productive days and days per 10,000 ft of drilling), but apparently no reference was made to the possibility of a blowout and questions of well control.[22]

Second, they would have reminded themselves (if necessary, asked for a briefing) about the controls that were supposed to be in place to prevent such events, and they would have made a mental note that, should circumstances allow, they would seek to verify that one or more of these controls was working as intended.

Third, just as executives on this occasion briefed themselves beforehand on previous occupational safety incidents on other rigs with a view to seeing whether lessons had been transferred, they would have briefed themselves on previous well safety incidents, for the same reason. In this case, the North Sea incident, four months earlier, would have led them to pay particular attention to whether the rig was monitoring the fluid flows in and out of the Macondo well.

Fourth, regardless of the North Sea blowout, given the fundamental importance of mud monitoring for the safety of the well, at least one of the visitors would have dedicated himself to observing this process. He would have discovered that it was not happening, and would have raised the matter immediately with the installation manager.

Fifth, they would have inquired beforehand about what would be happening on the rig while they were there, so as to be able to take advantage of any particular auditing opportunities that might arise. They would have discovered that the rig would be pressure testing the well. As a result, at least one of the visitors would have decided to monitor this testing process closely. They would have asked people to explain at every step along the way what they were doing. This is certainly an interventionist approach, but it is not necessarily a disruption or distraction to what is going on. Indeed, it may focus attention more effectively on what is going on. Sometimes this may slow activities down, but that is surely the prerogative of a senior manager, and it may be a necessary price to pay if managers are to assure themselves that all is in order.

Sixth, had the executives not been expert drillers, they might not have been in a position to understand what was going on. In such circumstances, it would have been appropriate to include an expert drilling engineer in the party who might have acted almost as an interpreter for the visitors. The high status of the visitors, coupled with the expertise of the "interpreter", make this a surprisingly effective auditing strategy.*

Senior executives visiting hazardous worksites would be well advised to adopt the auditing strategy just outlined, in addition to, or perhaps even in place of, asking questions about occupational injury. That is the enduring lesson from the *Deepwater Horizon* management walk-around.

Eliciting staff concerns

Discussion so far has focused primarily on one of the purposes of management walk-arounds, namely, informal auditing and the need to focus this on the major hazard management system. This depends on executives having a clear idea of how that system is supposed to work, and probing to see if it is working as intended. It is a relatively directed process of inquiry.

The other major purpose identified at the start of this chapter was described as eliciting staff concerns. This approach is well developed in the healthcare field where it involves asking a series of broad, open-ended questions designed to get people to speak freely about the impact that senior management strategies are having on them. This is about listening, rather than auditing.

---

* I once had the experience of doing an informal audit of compliance by electricity line workers. I did not know what I was observing but I was accompanied by an expert who understood very well what was going on and, in the course of one morning, we discovered several cases of unsafe behaviour arising essentially from inadequate procedures.

There is another way of thinking about this listening strategy in major hazard industries. Prior to every disaster, there are always warning signs — indications that things are amiss. Had these signs been identified earlier, the disaster could have been avoided. It is also true that people at the grass roots of an organisation are frequently aware of what is happening but do not transmit the bad news upwards, for a variety of reasons.

One of the most important reasons is an attitude on the part of senior management that discourages the reporting of bad news. BP's CEO at the time of the Texas City accident created a climate in which bad news was not welcome.[23] Likewise, the head of BP's exploration and production division at the time of the Macondo accident "was not someone people wanted to share bad news with".[24]

All of this is something that high reliability organisations are acutely aware of. For them, bad news is good news because it means that their communication systems are working to move the bad news up the hierarchy to the point where something can be done about it before it is too late.

Mindful leaders exhibit a "chronic unease" about whether they are getting the information they need.[25] One such leader I met had embarked on a campaign to "encourage the escalation of bad news". I sat in her office one day while she was talking on the phone to a lower-level manager who had provided her with a report that presented only good news. "But where is the bad news", she said. "I want you to rewrite your report to include the bad news." The organisation in question had a policy of "challenging the green and embracing the red". The slogan referred specifically to traffic light score cards, but it also had the more metaphorical meaning of questioning the good news and welcoming the bad. She was implementing this slogan in a very effective way.

She had also introduced an incentive system to encourage the reporting of bad news. Whenever someone demonstrated courage in transmitting bad news upwards, she provided them with an award (named after a man in her organisation who had saved someone's life by his alertness to a process safety hazard). The award had various levels, the highest being diamond which was worth $1,000. The day that I sat in her office, she made a diamond award to an operator who had recognised that some alarm levels had been changed on a rotary compressor without a proper management of change procedure. He had written an email about this to his manager who, in turn, had passed it on to her. She had made more than a hundred awards for courageous reporting in a period of less than 12 months.

Against this background, let me return to the issue of walk-arounds. Mindful leaders will treat their walk-arounds as an opportunity to seek out and listen to the bad news. One of the audit reports prior to the Texas City Refinery disaster put it well: senior managers, it said, needed to "listen to the voice of the refinery".

Had they done so, they would have discovered how time pressures and cost cuts were compromising process safety.

Listening in this way does not always come easily, and many companies provide their executives with prompt cards listing questions that they might ask. Some are better than others. Here is one set of questions designed to get people to open up and to give voice to any concerns that they may have:

- Tell me about your job. What do you do?
- What could go wrong? What are the greatest dangers you face?
- Do you think we have these dangers sufficiently under control?
- Do you think there are any safety issues here that we are not dealing with adequately?
- Are there times when workers feel they need to take short cuts?

These are open-ended questions aimed at promoting a conversation and, in this respect, they are rather different from the audit-type questions described earlier.[26]

Two final points. This kind of exercise calls for some level of humility on the part of the leaders because the whole purpose of the interaction is to learn from workers. Second, the chances of real communication will be maximised if the interaction is one-to-one. This means that leaders need to do their walk-arounds by themselves and, in particular, they should not be accompanied by a local manager who may inadvertently distort the communication.

Discussion

Let us consider the strengths and weaknesses of the two investigative strategies discussed above — auditing and listening. The major hazard auditing strategy is relatively focused and therefore does not, in itself, provide an opportunity for workers to talk about other things that may be troubling them and that may impact on major hazard safety.

On the other hand, the listening strategy looks at things from the worker's point of view. Where work practices have drifted away from written policy and procedure, workers may be unaware of this. Hence, it will not come up in ordinary conversation, and directed, audit-style questions may be necessary to detect this discrepancy.

It must also be noted that the listening strategy depends on workers and executives having a common language, literally. Many multinational energy companies are using workforces that don't speak the language of their executive managers, and it is impossible for any real communication to occur in these circumstances. However, the auditing strategy does not depend to the same extent on conversations with frontline workers. Questions about barriers that are supposed to be in place may be better addressed to more senior site staff and to control room operators, who are more likely to speak the language of their executive managers.

The question that remains to be addressed is whether or not these two strategies are incompatible. They will be, if audit-type questions leave employees feeling vulnerable. They will then not feel comfortable about raising other concerns. However, auditing does not necessarily make individuals feel vulnerable. In many situations, employees are not following written procedures because they regard them as inapplicable or unworkable. Moreover, they will probably be able to articulate this quite persuasively. It may also be that the procedural non-compliance is endorsed either explicitly or implicitly by local managers. In such a situation, people are behaving in accordance with "the way we do things around here", that is, in accordance with the local culture, and they are likely to be quite open about it.* Asking questions about this will not necessarily discourage them from raising other issues.

I conclude from this that these two purposes — auditing and listening — are not so inconsistent that managers need to choose and restrict themselves to one or the other. They can certainly do both during the same visit, although perhaps not in the same conversation. The main point is that executives need to be clear about which of the two purposes they are pursuing at any one time. They may in fact be able to pursue both, almost simultaneously.

Chapter

9

---

* The failure to monitor the Macondo well after it had been tested and declared safe is an example of this type of locally emergent culture, which rig staff felt no need to hide. See Chapter 4.

Endnotes

1   J Loud, "Walking the talk: safety management by walking around", paper presented in Albuquerque, New Mexico, in August 2006 at the 24th International System Safety Conference. See also Buckner, 2008; Frankel, 2008; Peters and Waterman, 1982.

2   King, 2012.

3   DWI, 23 August, p 446.

4   DWI, 29 May, p 172. The *Deepwater Horizon* was a floating vessel that was kept in position by multiple propellers in a process known as dynamic positioning.

5   DWI, 27 May, p 198.

6   DWI, 29 May, p 187.

7   DWI, 26 August, p 362.

8   DWI, 24 August, p 193.

9   DWI, 26 August, p 136.

10 DWI, 24 August, p 78. Later, in testimony, he denied that personnel were confused (DWI, 24 August, p 200).

11 DWI, 24 August, p 200.

12 DWI, 23 August, p 443.

13 DWI, 26 August, p 445.

14 *Wall Street Journal*, 17 August 2010, "Safety warning preceded rig blast".

15 DWI, 24 August, p 120.

16 DWI, 25 August, p 156.

17 DWI, 25 August, p 88.

18 DWI, 29 May, p 190.

19 DWI, 22 July, Rostho, p 7.

20 DWI, 26 May, Rose, p 450.

21 DWI, 7 December, Keith, pp 79-83.

22 DWI, 26 August, p 157.

23 Hopkins, 2008, ch 11.

24 Bergin, 2011, p 123 (see also p 102).

25 Hopkins, 2008, p 113.

26 These questions are discussed in Hopkins, 2008, ch 11.

CHAPTER 10

REGULATION

The regulatory regime for offshore petroleum safety came under withering criticism after the Macondo accident. There is an irony here. A blowout and massive oil spill occurred in Australian waters some nine months before Macondo, and industry sources in the United States were saying just weeks before the Macondo blowout that such an accident could never happen in the Gulf of Mexico because of superior regulation in the US.[1] However, post-Macondo scrutiny of the US system has shown it to be sadly deficient, and many commentators have since urged the US to adopt a safety case regime,* such as exists in the coastal waters of the United Kingdom, Norway, and even Australia![2] The Presidential Oil Spill Commission devoted a great deal of attention to identifying the most appropriate system of regulation for the US and came out strongly in favour of the safety case proposal.[3] However, the political realities in the US make it unlikely that this recommendation will be adopted in the foreseeable future.

This chapter identifies some of the reasons for the limited effectiveness of the pre-Macondo US regime. It shows, among other things, that there was an "unhealthy co-dependence" between the regulator and the regulated. It examines some of the characteristics of the safety case regulatory model and argues that the post-Macondo regulatory reforms fall a long way short of this ideal. Finally, it makes some recommendations about how existing safety case regimes can be improved.

Criticisms of the pre-Macondo system can be conveniently divided into two broad groups — criticisms of the regulator and criticisms of the regulations that it enforced. These will be dealt with below, in turn.

The regulator

The regulator at the time was known as the Minerals Management Service (MMS). The effectiveness of the MMS as a safety regulator was severely compromised by a fundamental conflict of interest. It was charged not only with ensuring compliance with environmental and safety regulations, but also with the sale of leases and the collection of revenue. This revenue was enormously important. By the 1980s, it was the second largest revenue source for the US Treasury.[4] Not surprisingly,

---

* This term will be defined later.

the revenue-maximising function was paramount, and the enforcement of safety regulations was compromised in various ways.[5]

In retrospect, the problem was so obvious that, within just two months of the accident,[6] the government abolished the MMS and created a separate safety regulator. However, the new regulator remains administratively part of the same department, the Department of the Interior, and debate continues as to just how independent it can be in this location.

This whole issue of regulatory independence has a long history. In the case of the offshore petroleum industry, it was highlighted in the Cullen inquiry following the Piper Alpha disaster off the coast of Scotland in 1988, in which 167 men died. The inquiry examined the role of the regulator at the time, the UK Department of Energy, and found it to be compromised in exactly the same way as the MMS. As a result, the safety function of the Department of Energy was transferred to the UK Health and Safety Executive, a dedicated safety agency responsible for all workplace safety.

Many of the lessons of Piper Alpha have been learnt by companies and by governments around the world, but this very important lesson on the need for regulatory independence did not make it across the Atlantic. Tragically, the US needed to have its own equivalent of Piper Alpha before such a change would become politically possible.[7] It is clear that governments, as well as companies, have difficulty learning lessons.*

For safety regulators to function effectively, they need independence not just from the revenue collecting arm of government. They need to be insulated from the political process. The Presidential Commission captured this in the following comment:[8]

> "The root of the problem has ... been that political leaders within both the Executive Branch and Congress have failed to ensure that the agency regulators have had the resources necessary to exercise [the government's] authority, including personnel and technical expertise, and, no less important, the political autonomy needed to overcome the powerful commercial interests that have opposed more stringent safety regulation."

---

* The reality is that the US Government is not in a position to learn from incidents like Piper Alpha. Its policy decisions are severely circumscribed by what is politically possible. It took a disaster of the magnitude of Macondo to make possible the changes that have occurred. The political circumstances preclude more far-reaching change. On the paralysis of the US political system, see www.laprogressive.com/elections/political-process-haunted-paralysis/ and the many references therein.

This statement identifies two ways in which the political process undermined the effectiveness of the regulatory function: first, by starving the agency of resources,[9] and second, by influencing regulatory rule-making. The Commission provides two examples of this influence on rule-making that are directly relevant to the themes of this book. First, as discussed in Chapter 6, offshore safety depends on identifying relevant measures, or metrics, and making them matter. One of the metrics, recognised around the world as important, is the number of gas releases. If this number can be driven down, the risk of major accident in production operations is correspondingly reduced. Accordingly, in 2003, the MMS tried to update its requirements for the reporting of key risk indicators. It proposed a rule that *all* unintentional gas releases be reported, because even small releases can lead to explosions. As chronicled by the Presidential Commission,[10] the White House "stiffly opposed" these efforts, and industry "vehemently objected that the requirement would be too burdensome and not conducive to safety". The MMS lost the battle and, in the end, could only require that gas releases be reported if they resulted in "equipment or process shutdown",[11] a very much smaller category of gas releases.

The second example of political interference concerns an attempt by the MMS to implement one of the most important lessons from the Piper Alpha disaster. This was that detailed prescriptive rules designed by the regulator were not sufficient to ensure safety in hazardous industries. What was required, in addition, was that companies take responsibility themselves for identifying the particular hazards that they face and for devising appropriate ways to manage those hazards. Accordingly, in 1991, the MMS proposed that industry should be required to develop "safety and environmental management plans" similar to those being developed in the UK. Such plans would require companies to identify hazards and specify how they intended to control them. What happened next is well described by the Presidential Commission:[12]

> "The agency's efforts to adopt a more rigorous and effective risk-based safety regulatory regime were repeatedly revisited, refined, delayed, and blocked alternatively by industry or sceptical political appointees. MMS thus never achieved the reform of its regulatory oversight of drilling safety consonant with practices that most other countries had embraced decades earlier."*

At the time of the Macondo incident, then, the MMS was still operating with a set of regulations that were "frozen in time", to use the Commission's turn of phrase.[13]

Chapter
10

---

* This is a reference to the safety case regimes adopted by many other jurisdictions around the world.

Only after the Macondo incident did the MMS's successor, BOEMRE,[14] finally make it mandatory that companies implement a "safety and environmental management system" (SEMS).[15] Industry had previously objected that:

- "the safety and environmental protection record of the offshore industry is excellent and that imposing these new requirements in not justified";
- "BOEMRE significantly underestimated the cost of developing, revising and implementing the SEMS program"; and
- "BOEMRE dramatically underestimated the major new documentation and reporting burden that the rule will impose on offshore operators".[16]

In the post-Macondo environment, these objections were swept away, and the new rule was one of a number promulgated by the newly energised regulator.

The limitations of prescriptive rules

The MMS had developed a voluminous set of rules with which operators were required to comply. Some were quite generally worded, for example:

- You must take necessary precautions to keep wells under control at all times.[17]
- The lessee shall not create conditions that will pose unreasonable risk to public health, life, property ... [18]
- You must protect health, safety, property, and the environment by performing all operations in a safe and workmanlike manner ...[19]

Precisely because of their generality, these rules are open to interpretation and they do not offer clear guidance to regulators engaged in routine inspections. Rather than trying to use these rules to maximum advantage, inspectors focused on hardware-specific rules, where compliance or non-compliance was easier to determine. In particular, the focus was on whether certain items of equipment were being tested at the requisite frequency. This was easily ascertainable from the paperwork. To this end, the MMS had compiled a list of "potential items of non-compliance" (PINCs) and inspectors generally confined themselves to doing checks against this list. The rationale for using such a list was that it ensured that the agency's inspection program was consistent,[20] but it also meant that inspectors needed very little expertise to carry out their inspections.[21] For an agency starved of resources, this was a significant benefit.

This inspection strategy had major drawbacks. First, operators knew what was on the list of potential non-compliances and focused their attention on these items. Regulatory requirements that were not on this restricted list tended to be overlooked. A good example of this was the requirement that the operator conduct a major inspection of blowout preventer (BOP) components every three to five years. This was not included on the PINC checklist, so inspectors did not regularly verify compliance with this requirement.[22] At the time of the Macondo incident, the BOP had not in fact been inspected with the requisite frequency.[23]

More importantly, these hardware-related PINCs completely ignored the human and organisational factors that play a major role in every accident — and certainly played a part in the Macondo accident. In particular, MMS inspectors paid no attention to whether or not operators were complying with well control procedures.

This limitation is dramatically illustrated by the fact that the *Deepwater Horizon* was visited by MMS inspectors on three occasions in the two months prior to the accident, and in not one of these did they find an incident of non-compliance worthy of reporting.[24] The fact that the *Deepwater Horizon* could pass these inspections with flying colours, yet fail "Well Control 101", as some commentators have put it, highlights the failure of the MMS inspection strategy.

A further limitation of the purely prescriptive approach is that it means that regulators are always playing catch up. Prior to the Macondo incident, the largest ever oil spill in the US resulted from the holing of a tanker, the *Exxon Valdez*. Legislators responded with the Oil Pollution Act of 1990, requiring oil spill response plans. The Act also introduced a requirement for double-hull tankers, a measure specifically designed to reduce the risk of oil tanker spills. No attention was paid to other ways in which oil spills might occur. So it was that, at the time of the Macondo incident, there were no specific regulatory requirements to be able to cap and contain blowouts effectively. To avoid being always one step behind in this way, what is needed is legislation or regulations that require operators to identify *all* major accident events and, as far as practicable, to put in place controls to deal with all of them.

Related to this is the fact that government-imposed prescriptive rules do not and cannot cover every situation. In particular, "MMS regulations in force at the time of the Macondo blowout did not address many of the key issues that the Chief Counsel's team identified as risk factors for the blowout".[25] This is not to say that governments should try to promulgate detailed regulations that cover every aspect of operations; it is probably impossible to do that. It is better to rely on an enforceable general duty of care, to be discussed below.

Chapter

10

Losing sight of safety

The MMS approach was one that encouraged operators to see the ultimate goal as regulatory compliance, not the safety of the operation. In fact, it discouraged them from taking a broader view of their safety responsibilities. This is a controversial claim, so I shall offer several examples by way of demonstration.

First, as we saw in Chapter 4, the lack of any strategy in BP's exploration plan to deal with a blowout was justified on the grounds that BP was not required by the regulator to have such a strategy. Apparently, there was no incentive at all for BP to go beyond what was explicitly required by the regulator.

Second, consider the way that BOPs were tested. There are many types of test that can be done on a complex piece of equipment such as a BOP. The ultimate test is to ask it to perform its emergency function in circumstances that are as close as possible to those that will prevail in the emergency. This is time-consuming and expensive. A study done for the regulator in 2002 found that, of six BOPs that were tested in this way, only three succeeded in shearing the drill pipe. This is a failure rate of 50%.[26] It is also possible to test individual components of a BOP without calling on it to cut through pipe in the conditions that exist on the sea floor. An example would be testing whether electrical circuits are functioning as intended. The regulator required a large number of such tests which were nearly always successful — there were only 62 failures out of 90,000 tests conducted over several years.[27] In short, while realistic testing of BOP ability to function in an emergency yielded an alarming failure rate of 50%, the more limited forms of testing prescribed by the regulator suggested that BOPs functioned in a very reliable way. This discrepancy seemed not to matter, however, because what was uppermost in everyone's mind was regulatory compliance, not safety. The testing regime had lost sight of safety. One is reminded of the drunk who searched for his car keys under a street light (even though that was not where he had lost them), simply because that was where it was easiest to see.[28] In the same way, tests were prescribed because they were relatively easy to do, not because they could provide the ultimate demonstration that a BOP would function as intended in an emergency.

Here is a third example of the way in which the MMS approach fostered what some have called a "compliance mentality", that is, a mentality in which the ultimate goal is regulatory compliance, not the safety of the operation. According to BP standards, the cementing operation should seek to push cement up the annulus to 1,000 ft above the oil and gas sand layers. In other words, the standards envisaged a 1,000 ft safety margin against the possibility of a blowout occurring up the annulus (see Figure 10.1).

The MMS requirement was 500 ft above the pay zone, while the industry standard specified only 10 ft![29]

BP engineers had a particular reason not to fill the annulus to the full 1,000 ft, and they had sought and obtained a dispensation from their own standard from the BP engineering authority. The dispensation allowed them to adopt the MMS standard of 500 ft. However, they knew that, if they did not get full returns, that is, if some of the cement disappeared into the pay sands, they might not achieve the 500 ft

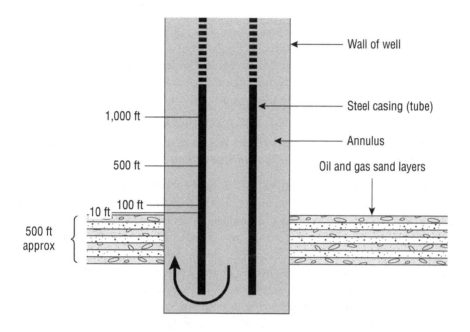

FIGURE 10.1: Possible top of cement levels above top of pay sands

safety margin. The decision was therefore made — it is recorded in the decision tree in Appendix 1 — that 100 ft might be enough. If there was some loss of returns but *estimates* suggested that the cement had reached at least 100 ft above the pay zone, then the Macondo team would seek a further dispensation from BP standards and also an authorisation from the MMS to dispense with the MMS requirement.

The figure of 100 ft was not the result of any risk assessment that the engineers had carried out themselves. According to BP's standards, 100 ft was acceptable if the position of the top of the cement was *established* with a proven cement evaluation technique, such as a cement bond log.[30] But the engineers were not proposing to use such a tool; the proposal was that, if the *estimate* (based on volume of lost returns) suggested that they had a safety margin of at least 100 ft, they would be satisfied, and they would seek dispensation from both BP standards and the MMS requirements. This showed scant regard for BP's own standards. But the point in the present context is that it showed a decidedly opportunistic approach to the MMS standard. If the MMS could be persuaded to authorise a departure from its standards, that was enough for the Macondo team. Again, their purpose was to ensure that they were compliant, not that they were safe.

Chapter

10

The regulator generally approved such requests.[31] Moreover, the approval was usually granted quickly (within a few hours). One such request for variation was granted within 90 minutes![32] Given that there was only one person performing this function in the MMS regional office,[33] it is highly doubtful that the approval process was much more than a rubber stamp. In fact, the approver relied on what was said in applications and rarely asked questions.[34]

Where each party relies on the other in this way, no one really takes responsibility. It is for this reason that the process has been described by knowledgeable commentators as one of "unhealthy co-dependence".[35]

At the risk of labouring the point, here is one final example. With drilling completed, there was some left-over well fluid on the deck of the *Deepwater Horizon*. To take this back to shore was going to incur additional expense. BP therefore had an interest in dumping it overboard. But this would have constituted a reportable environmental incident and was therefore unacceptable. At the same time, the team needed to pump some spacer fluid into the well, as part of the normal operation. This fluid would eventually return to the surface and, under existing regulations, it could be pumped directly into the ocean, without constituting a reportable environmental incident. The decision was made, therefore, to use the left-over fluid as spacer fluid, and to use all of it, even though there was twice as much as was necessary, so that it would all finish up in the ocean, thereby avoiding disposal costs. The proposal was scrutinised by on-shore personnel to ensure that it complied with environmental rules, but it was not scrutinised for its impact on safety. As it turns out, the extra fluid that was used may have blocked one of the lines used for the reduced pressure test, and thereby contributed to the misinterpretation of the test results.[36] But the possibility that this might happen was not considered. In this way, BP's concern with cost, coupled with its focus on regulatory compliance to the exclusion of all else, may well have contributed to the blowout.

These examples demonstrate how BP tended to lose sight of safety and become focused on a kind of ritualistic compliance as a result of the prescriptive regime operated by the MMS.

A disclaimer — the need for rules

The preceding discussion has demonstrated the inadequacy of the prescriptive regulatory approach *as implemented by the MMS*. This is not an argument against prescriptive rules as such. Indeed, one of the clearest lessons emerging from the Macondo incident is the need for companies to develop rigorous procedures and standards and to ensure that they are complied with. In the face of complex hazards, people need rules to guide their behaviour since, as noted in Chapter 8, their own experience and expertise may not be enough to ensure safe operation.

But these rules need to operate within a framework that encourages risk awareness, not one that substitutes compliance for risk awareness, as the MMS framework did.[37]

Regulatory reform

The most widely made recommendation following the Macondo blowout was for the introduction of a safety case regime. Such regimes have evolved in many jurisdictions around the world. However, they are not readily transplanted from one jurisdiction to another because they depend on various political and legal pre-conditions. In this section, I want to highlight four basic features of a successful safety case regime and identify some of the ways in which the post-Macondo regime in the US falls short of this model. The four features are:

(1) a risk management framework;

(2) a requirement to "make the case" to the regulator;

(3) a competent and independent regulator; and

(4) a general duty of care imposed on the operator.

A risk management framework

A safety case regime requires companies to adopt a systematic risk management framework. In particular, it requires them to identify all major hazards and to develop plans for how these hazards will be managed. This is very similar to the post-Macondo requirement that companies in US waters develop a SEMS.

A requirement to "make the case" to the regulator

Notwithstanding the above similarity, the SEMS approach falls short of a safety case in important respects. A safety case is a *case* — an argument made to the regulator. Companies must demonstrate to the regulator the processes they have gone through to identify hazards, the methodology they have used to assess risks, and the reasoning that has led them to choose one control rather than another. Finally, the regulator must accept (or reject) the case.

The new US rule provides no such licensing or approval role for the regulator. Indeed, SEMS documents do not even need to be lodged with the regulator. Guidance documents state that the regulator or its representative may evaluate or visit a facility to determine whether a "SEMS program is in place, addresses all the required elements and is effective ...".[38] Facilities to be evaluated in this way may be chosen at random or on the basis of performance. This is a long way short of the oversight provided under a safety case regime.

A safety case does not give operators a free rein in how they respond to hazards. They need to specify the procedures and standards that they intend to adopt. Where an operator proposes to adopt an inadequate standard, a safety case regulator may challenge the operator to adopt a better standard. The Presidential Commission noted that American Petroleum Industry standards are "lowest common denominator", not best industry practice. It argued that the US regulatory regime was undermined by the fact that the regulator relies on these standards.[39] A safety case regulator in these circumstances can challenge the operator to adopt the best international standards. However, the success of this challenge may depend on whether or not the jurisdiction imposes a general duty on the operator to manage risk effectively (see below), which would, in effect, mandate that operators adopt the best international standards. The Presidential Commission circumvented this issue by recommending that the best international standards should be simply imposed on operators, without any room for them to argue for lesser standards.[40]

A competent and independent regulator

Many jurisdictions around the world have fallen into the trap of thinking that all they need to do to institute a safety case regime is enact the necessary legislation. This is a serious error. Safety case regimes have only functioned well when there is a competent and independent regulator. The initial process of evaluating and accepting (or rejecting) a safety case requires a high level of expertise if it is not to degenerate into a rubber stamp exercise.

A dramatic illustration of how a safety case regime will fail in the absence of a competent and independent regulator is provided by the crash of a British Air Force Nimrod in Afghanistan in 2006.[41] The Air Force had prepared a safety case for the Nimrod which was totally inadequate and failed to identify the hazards that led to the crash. The safety case was not presented to an external regulator and was not subjected to independent challenge.[42] It was approved internally, without scrutiny, at a "customer acceptance conference". As a result, its many errors and deficiencies went unnoticed. The accident review excoriated the Nimrod safety case as "a lamentable job from start to finish", and concluded that those responsible for it displayed "incompetence, complacency and cynicism".[43] The point is that, without scrutiny by an independent regulator, a safety case may not be worth the paper it is written on.

A safety case regime also changes what it is that regulators must do when they make site visits. Rather than inspecting to ensure that hardware is working, or that documents are up to date, they must audit against the safety case to ensure that the specified controls are functioning as intended. The outcome of any risk management process can be summarised in a bowtie diagram, or a series of such diagrams, as discussed in Chapter 4. A good auditor will therefore find it useful to study the bowtie diagrams and check whether the controls indicated in these diagrams are indeed in place. Auditing in this way breathes life into safety case documents. Unless regulators are willing and able to do this, a safety case may be no more than a lifeless set of documents sitting on some inaccessible shelf, gathering dust. However, such auditing requires a sophisticated understanding of accident causation and prevention, which in turn means that safety case regulators need a higher level of education than was the case for MMS inspectors, who normally had only high school education.

Offshore safety case regulators around the world have sometimes been set up under a special Act of the legislature to be independent of the executive arm of government, that is, not subject to ministerial control. A Presidential Commission staff working paper recommended exactly that for the US.[44] It argued that the agency would need its own "organic Act", that is, a statute enacted by Congress to create the agency and define its powers. Moreover, the director would need to have a fixed-term appointment and be appointed for his or her technical expertise. The paper suggested that, so as not to be at the mercy of a Congressional appropriation system, the agency should be funded directly by a levy on industry, a strategy that is already in place for some peer regulators. Among other things, this would enable the regulator to pay salaries comparable to those available in industry, so as to be able to recruit and retain competent staff.

In making this set of recommendations, the working paper took its lead from a statement made to the Presidential Commission by the head of Shell Upstream in the US:[45]

> "The industry needs a robust, expertly staffed, and well-funded regulator that can keep pace with and augment industry's technical expertise. A competent and nimble regulator will be able to establish and enforce the rules of the road to assure safety without stifling innovation and commercial success."

The Presidential Commission endorsed these ideas and recommended the establishment of a statutory agency, to be known as the Offshore Safety Authority.[46] However, the Commission also recommended that the Authority be located "within" the Department of the Interior. This was not envisaged in the original staff working paper and potentially threatens the independence of the Authority.

At the time of writing, Congress had not acted on the recommendation to create an independent statutory authority. The regulator, the Bureau of Safety and Environmental Enforcement, remains an integral part of the Department of the Interior, created by order of the Secretary of the Department,[47] not by the legislature. Apparently, even after the Macondo accident, it is still politically impossible to do what is needed to create a truly competent and independent regulator.

Chapter

10

A general duty of care

Most safety case regimes are supported by legislation that imposes a general duty on the operator to reduce risks "as low as reasonably practicable", or words to that effect. This has important consequences. First, it provides leverage for regulators. If an operator wishes to adopt a procedure or a standard that falls short of good or best practice, the regulator can reject it on the grounds that is does not reduce the risk as low as reasonably practicable. This additional leverage is the reason that fire protection standards on rigs in UK waters are higher than for those in the Gulf of Mexico.[48]

Second, the general duty is, in effect, a duty to do whatever is reasonably practicable to identify and control all hazards. An operator cannot claim to be in compliance just because it has gone through a hazard identification process, if that process is demonstrably inadequate and fails to identify and control hazards that a reasonable operator would have identified and controlled. This makes it relatively easy to prosecute companies for a violation of their general duty after a Macondo-style event.

Third, the general duty means that, even if there is no directly applicable rule, operators still have a duty to manage risk. They must therefore maintain some reasonable level of risk awareness that goes beyond mere compliance. It is the general duty of care that raises a safety case regime above the blind compliance mentality that characterised the MMS regime.

Interestingly, there *is* a general duty specified under the Outer Continental Shelf Lands Act (OCSLA) under which the US regulator operates. Section 1348(b) states:[49]

> "It shall be the duty of any holder of a lease or permit under this subchapter to —
>
> (1) maintain all places of employment ... in compliance with occupational safety and health standards and, in addition, *free from recognized hazards to employees* ..." (emphasis added)

However, this overarching general duty to maintain the workplace free from recognised hazards appears to be a dead letter. The regulator's report on the Macondo incident identifies violations of specific regulatory requirements, but it does not suggest that section 1348(b) has been violated.[50] And the subsequent citations issued to the companies concerned are for specific regulatory violations, not for a violation of the general duty. If the general duty in the Act is not relevant in this context, it is hard to imagine any circumstances in which it might be invoked.

Summary

The preceding discussion identifies four elements of a safety case regime: a risk-based regulatory framework; a requirement to make the case for safety to the regulator; a competent and independent regulator; and an operator general duty of care. The four are inter-dependent and a functioning safety case regime requires all four. The post-Macondo US regulatory regime has introduced a requirement for a risk-based SEMS, but the other three elements are lacking. From this point of view, the window of opportunity provided by the Macondo disaster has been missed.

Improving the effectiveness of safety case regimes

While the safety case strategy is generally accepted as an improvement on purely prescriptive regimes, there remains room for improvement. Many major accident investigations in recent years have identified a variety of *organisational* factors that have contributed to the accident. In some respects, these can be regarded as root causes. On the whole, however, safety case regimes do not focus on these factors and operators therefore ignore them in their safety cases. My colleague, Jan Hayes, argues that it is time that safety case regimes around the world embraced this organisational perspective and challenged companies to demonstrate that they have thought hard about these issues.[51] Several of these organisational factors have come to light in this investigation and it is worth discussing here how they might be incorporated into a safety case framework.

Organisational design

In Chapter 7, we saw that engineers in BP's Gulf of Mexico operations reported in to operations managers at a relatively low level. Inevitably, this compromised their work. As BP itself recognised after the Macondo accident, engineering integrity depends on separating engineers from operations and making them answerable to more senior engineers. Ideally, these engineering lines should run to the top of the corporation, so as to maximise the independence of engineers from commercial pressures. Similarly, health and safety managers need to report up their own reporting line if they are to wield the greatest influence.[52]

Functional lines of this nature provide "services" to operations and so there needs to be dotted lines from functional to operational positions, as described in Chapter 7. This can complicate matters and takes us into the realm of a matrix organisational structure, which will not be discussed here.[53] But, as long as it is clear that the primary reporting lines for functional specialists are functional, not operational, this should minimise ambiguities.

There can be no single organisational structure that fits all circumstances, so it is not appropriate to lay down prescriptive rules. But safety case regulators should

Chapter

10

challenge companies to demonstrate how their organisational structures will ensure engineering integrity and, more generally, the autonomy of the safety function. Where companies adopt a decentralised structure such as BP had, it would be appropriate for safety case regulators to challenge whether the risks are as low as reasonably practicable, and such companies would need to demonstrate carefully how their structure delivered the same benefits as a more centralised structure. One of BP's responses to the Macondo incident was to set up a powerful central agency to audit and, if necessary, intervene in technical activities, and one could imagine a company that was decentralised with respect to engineering services defending itself by reference to such a centralised auditing function. Whether or not this is a satisfactory solution is not the point here. The point is that opening up the whole issue of organisational structure to regulatory scrutiny and discussion could be expected to have beneficial effects. Safety case regulators could ultimately find themselves advising on good organisational design and developing codes of practice in this area.

Performance measures

BP, Transocean and others had demonstrated an admirable commitment to personal safety. The walk-around described in Chapter 9 revealed that managers were serious about minimising the risk of personal injury. Injury statistics, both recordable injuries and lost-time injury rates, played a substantial role in generating this concern. These statistics were highly visible, and bonuses were in part determined by how successful companies were in driving or keeping down these injury rates. This was a measure that truly mattered. Of course, this provided an incentive to manipulate the statistics, but it also provided an incentive to minimise risk, as was clearly evidenced in the walk-around.

The challenge is to find measures of how well *major* hazards are being managed and to make them matter in the same way. Here is where regulators can play a vital role. As noted in Chapter 6, appropriate measures of major hazard risk management in the drilling industry would include numbers of kicks, speed of response to well kicks, numbers of cement failures, and perhaps numbers of times gas alarms are triggered. All of these numbers would need to be refined in relevant ways to provide appropriate indicators. Regulators should require the reporting of such precursor events, and find ways to make these measures matter, for example, by making company-specific data publicly available.[54] This will encourage companies to pay the same attention to major hazards or process safety as is currently being paid to personal safety. Using performance measurement in this way encourages companies to work out for themselves how best to manage major accident risk, rather than relying on regulators to figure it out for them. This is the essence of the safety case approach.

Incentive systems

As noted above, senior management incentive systems often contain a component that reflects how well personal safety is being managed. They also need to incorporate measures of how well process safety or major hazards are being managed. This is not straightforward. We saw in Chapter 6 that BP had tried to do this, but had failed to target the hazards that confront the drilling industry. Safety case regulators should raise questions about the remuneration systems used by companies and the extent to which they encourage companies to manage their major hazards effectively. They should challenge companies to demonstrate that their incentive systems are appropriately focused.

For senior executives, incentive systems are embodied in performance agreements. These agreements are generally regarded as personal and therefore confidential. Yet they can be very public in their consequences and should therefore be subject to external scrutiny, in the public interest.

Incorporating lessons learnt into safety cases[55]

One of the most striking findings of major accident inquiries is the way that the organisations concerned had failed to learn from previous incidents, both internal and external to the organisation.

Safety case regulators could easily require that safety cases demonstrate how lessons from previous relevant incidents have been identified and implemented. Operators in the oil and gas industry could be required to demonstrate what they had learnt from the Piper Alpha, Texas City or Macondo accidents, and how these lessons had been incorporated into their risk management system and/or organisational structure. This would be an extremely valuable exercise for all concerned.

Ongoing learning from incidents

Safety management systems, such as the new SEMS requirement for the US offshore oil and gas industry, usually contain a requirement that *internal* incidents be investigated and learnt from. But there is little detail on how this is to be done. Nor is there typically a requirement that organisations learn from relevant *externally* occurring incidents. Safety case regimes should require operators to demonstrate how they intend to learn from incidents, both internal and external, *as they occur*. We know that it is not enough to circulate bulletins about lessons learnt. The problem is to ensure that these lessons really are implemented. Companies should be required to explain in some detail in their safety case just how they intend to ensure that learning from incidents is effective. Putting this another way, many of these organisations claim to be learning organisations. Safety case regimes should challenge them to demonstrate that they are.

Conclusion

Major accidents are times of crisis, not only for the companies concerned, but also for the safety regulator. Frequently, such accidents reveal fundamental weaknesses in the regulatory regime. That was very much the case with the Macondo accident, and it led to calls from many quarters for the introduction of a safety case regime. This chapter has sought to sketch very briefly what is involved in such a regime and the ways in which it represents an improvement on the regulatory regime that existed at the time of the Macondo blowout. There can be no certainty that a safety case regime would have prevented this accident, but the kind of regime outlined above would have reduced its likelihood.

The weakness of the regulatory regime at the time of the Macondo blowout was a consequence of a lack of resolve at the political level to ensure effective regulation. It is only when an accident forces a shift in the balance of political forces that real change is possible. It is a depressing commentary on the US political system that the shock of the Macondo disaster has not been sufficient to shift the political balance in favour of a safety case regime.

The analysis of the Macondo incident presented in this book highlights organisational causes that are not adequately dealt with in most safety case regimes. The Macondo accident therefore provides an opportunity for regulators around the world to finetune their safety case regimes, regardless of what happens in the US.

Endnotes

1   See www.reefrelieffounders.com/drilling/2010/03/29/orlando-sentinel-could-oil-spill-disaster-happen-in-fla-aussie-rig-debacle-offers-lessons/. Walter Cruickshank, Deputy Director of the Minerals Management Service, told a congressional inquiry on 19 November 2009 that US government regulations would prevent a Montara-like blowout in the US (www.gpo.gov/fdsys/pkg/CHRG-111shrg55331/html/CHRG-111shrg55331.htm).

2   The Australian blowout revealed weaknesses in regulatory coverage, but it did not cast doubt on the safety case principles (*Report of the Montara Commission of Inquiry*, June 2010).

3   OSC, p 252.

4   OSC, p 63.

5   OSC, "A competent and nimble regulator: a new approach to risk assessment and management", staff working paper no. 21, p 17.

6   OSC, p 55.

7   This is the view of Magne Ognedal, Director General of the Norwegian Petroleum Safety Authority, quoted in "A competent and nimble regulator", op cit, p19.

8   OSC, p 67.

9   OSC, pp 72, 73.

10   OSC, p 72.

11   Federal Register, vol 71, no. 73, Monday, 17 April 2006, Rules and Regulations, p 19642.

12   OSC, p 71.

13   OSC, p 71.

14   Bureau of Ocean Energy Management, Regulation and Enforcement.

15   The new rule adopts API RP75.

16   Federal Register, Friday, 15 October 2010, vol 75, no. 199, Rules and Regulations, pp 63612, 63613. These objections were made in a comment period that closed on 15 September 2009.

17   30 CFR 250.401.

18   30 CFR 250.300.

19   30 CFR 250.107.

20   BOEMRE, p 162.

21   See L Eaton, S Power and R Gold, "Inspectors adrift in rig-safety push: outgunned by industry and outmatched by jobs, agency lags", *Wall Street Journal*, 3 December 2010.

22   BOEMRE, p 163.

23   There is no suggestion that this failure contributed to the incident (BOEMRE, p 151).

24   BOEMRE, p 164.

25   CCR, p 253.

26   West Engineering Services, *Mini shear study*, for MMS, December 2002. See *New York Times* oil spill documents.

27   Blowout prevention equipment reliability joint industry project. See *New York Times* oil spill documents.

28   A version of this story is told in Klein, 2009, p xiii.

29   This was the understanding of the Macondo team. Note that the estimate of the width of the pay zone in the diagram is taken from BP, 2010, p 54.

30   CCR, p 79; OSC, p 102; BOEMRE, pp 59, 60.

31   CSB, 26 October, Walz, p 69.

32   CCR, p 258.

33   CCR, p 152.

34   CCR, p 253.

35   D Pritchard and K Lacy, "Deepwater well complexity — the new domain", Deepwater Horizon Study Group working paper, January 2011, p 7.

36   CCR, p 160.

37   This issue is too complex to be dealt with here and I refer the interested reader to my paper on this topic, Hopkins, 2011.

38   30 CFR 250.1924.

39   OSC, p 225.

40   OSC, p 252.

41   Haddon-Cave, 2009.

42   The importance of this challenge function is discussed by Leveson, 2011.

43   Haddon-Cave, 2009, p 259.

44   OSC, "A competent and nimble regulator: a new approach to risk assessment and management", staff working paper no. 21.

45   Ibid, p 1.

Chapter

10

46   Ibid, p 257.

47   Order no. 3299, 19 May 2010.

48   See the widely circulated paper by Bill Campbell, former Shell auditor, "Analysis of cause of explosion on Deepwater Horizon, 24/6/2010", p 8.

49   This is reminiscent of the general duty imposed by section 5(a)(1) of the US Occupational Safety and Health Act to provide a workplace that is "free from recognized hazards that are causing or are likely to cause death or serious physical harm".

50   The nearest it gets to this more general approach is to suggest that 30 CFR 250.107, 250.300 and 250.401 were violated.

51   Jan Hayes, "A new policy direction in offshore safety regulation", working paper no. 84, at http://ohs.anu.edu.au/. I am indebted to Jan for the basic argument in this section.

52   See Hopkins, 2007.

53   See Hopkins, 2008, ch 10; and S Balu, Organisational design for hazardous industry, forthcoming PhD thesis, Australian National University.

54   Even post-Macondo, BOEMRE only mandates the reporting of injuries/illnesses and oil spills. None of the precursor events to blowout are mandatorily reportable (Federal Register, vol 75, no. 199, 15 October 2010, Rules and Regulations, p 63635).

55   See Hayes, op cit, sec 6.

CHAPTER 11

SOME POPULAR ACCOUNTS OF THE MACONDO ACCIDENT

The Macondo accident generated an almost unprecedented amount of popular writing — by journalists, environmentalists, academics and others. This work offers broad-brush explanations rather than detailed causal analysis. Some of these accounts were mentioned in the introduction to this book, where they were summarily dismissed. This chapter provides a more extended treatment and, in some cases, a more thorough critique.

Two general claims are considered:

- BP is a particularly reckless company; and
- deepwater drilling involves such complex technology that accidents are inevitable.

A reckless company

The first perspective focuses on the fact that the Macondo accident happened to BP, not to any of the other major petroleum companies.

It was suggested in Chapter 7 that this may have something to do with BP's organisational structure, which was more decentralised than that of any of the other majors. This meant that engineering considerations were more likely to be swamped by business pressures than was true for the other majors. This is also the central thesis in Bergin's *Spills and Spins: the Inside Story of BP.*

Journalists Reed and Fitzgerald come close to this explanation when they write:[1]

> "The company's corporate DNA is different from its competitors, where engineering principles dominate. BP is more of a financial culture."

Reed and Fitzgerald are correct in pointing to differences in the importance of engineering principles, but they don't appear to recognise that this is an outcome of organisational differences, and they retreat, instead, to the DNA metaphor.

In much of the popular writing, however, a simpler explanation prevails: BP was a reckless company, a rogue company. This is what distinguished it from the others.

According to one writer, BP was the "industry stepchild", a "perpetual industry outsider" and, in an even more dramatic turn of phrase:[2]

> "… something was terribly wrong inside BP. Beneath the green veneer lurked festering and fundamental problems …"

One of the arguments made in support of this kind of claim was that BP had a worse record of regulatory violations than other corporations. "BP had distinguished itself as one of the worst offenders in the industry", it was said.[3] Here is one of the best documented statements:[4]

> "Between mid-2007 and early 2010, BP single-handedly accounted for nearly half of all OSHA safety citations to the entire refining industry … The record was even more lopsided for the worst offences. BP received 69 citations for 'wilful' violations, defined as including 'intentional disregard for employee safety and health' — triple the number for all the rest of the companies in the refining industry, in combination. Most spectacularly, though, BP received 760 citations — out of a grand total of 761 for the entire industry — for 'egregious wilful' violations, or the worst violations of all, reflecting 'wilful and flagrant' violations of health and safety laws."

On the face of it, this is a powerful indictment. However, the imbalance is so extreme that it casts doubt on whether these figures can be taken at face value. The fact is that, after the Texas City Refinery disaster in 2005, the Occupational Safety and Health Administration (OSHA) targeted BP refineries in North America, particularly Texas City. The egregious violations mentioned above were all from Texas City and one other BP refinery. At least some of the imbalance — it is hard to say how much — is attributable to this targeting. It is important to recognise that, generally speaking, enforcement statistics reflect the activities of the enforcers as much as the activities of those who are the targets of enforcement. For example, where there are spikes in road traffic violation statistics, this is likely to reflect a policing blitz rather than any sudden change in the behaviour of drivers. Similarly, the number of OSHA citations is very sensitive to OSHA enforcement policy and to the resources devoted to enforcement. The figures cited above cannot therefore be taken at face value.

It is difficult to get data that enable us to make reliable comparisons among the oil company majors, but some comparative data are available. A 2010 study[5] used a composite health and safety measure based on the following indicators:

- fatalities (35% of score);
- injuries (15%);
- hydrocarbon spills (35%); and

- the track record of industrial violations (including accusations, litigations and fines).

Using this composite measure, BP was in the bottom quartile, but so too was Shell and Chevron, while ExxonMobil was in the second-bottom quartile.

The study also produced a broader indicator of "operations, health and safety". On the basis of this indicator, ExxonMobil joined Shell, Chevron and BP in the bottom quartile. Top quartile companies included BG, ConocoPhillips and Statoil. These are startling findings. No doubt they, too, have numerous imperfections. But they lead to very different conclusions about the relative performance of BP.

If we focus for a moment on ExxonMobil, simply because it is at the opposite end of the organisational design spectrum discussed in Chapter 7, the picture becomes yet more complicated:[6]

> "Since 2005, Exxon's been assessed millions of dollars in fines for pollution violations in states including Massachusetts, Louisiana and Maryland and for chemical leaks off the California coast. Exxon currently faces allegations from the Sierra Club and Environment Texas that its refinery complex in Baytown, Texas, has violated federal air pollution laws thousands of times over the past five years."

We should note, finally, the view of the head of the safety regulator, who said after the Macondo event that, on the whole, BP "didn't have a deeply flawed record offshore" and actually ranked "close to the top tier" of operators in the Gulf.[7]

I am not seeking to draw any conclusions about the relative performance of BP and ExxonMobil or, for that matter, any other oil and gas major. The point is simply that it is not at all clear from the data that BP is an industry outlier, or is qualitatively worse than its competitors. It would be extraordinarily difficult to assemble data that unequivocally demonstrated such a difference.

Another way in which popular writers have sought to demonstrate BP's rogue status is to point to its record of calamitous events. The Texas City Refinery disaster occurred in early 2005. Two events that severely damaged BP's reputation followed in quick succession. In late 2005, the massive Thunderhorse platform in the Gulf of Mexico nearly capsized due to a construction fault. In 2006, an Alaskan pipeline leaked oil as a result of inadequate maintenance. The leak caused the temporary closure of the pipeline, with significant disruption of oil supplies to the United States. Both of these events were attributed to BP's cost-cutting mentality.

Chapter

11

Enumerating such events does not, however, demonstrate that BP is worse than other oil and gas majors. Shell has had its fair share of reputation-damaging events. There is a whole website devoted to publicising them.[8] Moreover, as noted in earlier chapters, Shell had a blowout in the North Sea, similar in many ways to the Macondo incident, except that the blowout preventer worked. Had it not, Shell would have been in deep trouble. ExxonMobil has also experienced reputation-damaging events in recent years, such as the fire at the Fawley Refinery in the United Kingdom in 2007.[9] In short, cataloging BP's failures does not in itself establish that it is worse than all of the rest.

There are further features of the Macondo incident that are inconsistent with an explanation in terms of BP recklessness. As we have seen, a failure by Halliburton contributed to the incident, as did a failure by Transocean. This was not just a BP accident; it was an industry accident. As the Presidential Commission noted, the Macondo incident "place[s] in doubt the safety culture of the entire industry".[10] Of course, other oil majors have disputed this conclusion, but the evidence speaks for itself.

Finally, consider the oil spill response plan that BP had had approved by the regulator. This was written for BP by a consultant. As BP struggled to deal with the blowout, its CEO admitted that they "were making it up day to day".[11] One can conclude from this that the plan was irrelevant to the task that they faced.

In fact, the oil spill response plan was in some respects an example of what one writer has called a fantasy document — a document that companies produce to demonstrate to regulators and the public the way they would deal with a catastrophic event.[12] Perhaps the clearest evidence of the fantasy nature of this document is the mention of the need to protect sea lions, sea otters and walruses, none of which exist in the Gulf of Mexico.[13]

But the crucial and startling point is this: the same oil spill response plan, prepared by the same contractor, replete with the same references to marine mammals that don't exist in the Gulf, was being used by Chevron, ConocoPhillips, ExxonMobil and Shell![14] It would seem that these companies were just as unprepared to deal with a Macondo-style blowout as was BP. From this point of view, they were just as culpable as BP.

In summary, the popular view that the accident was the outcome of a uniquely reckless corporate culture is, to say the least, grossly overstated.

Technological inevitability

One of the persistent refrains in the popular literature was that a Macondo-style accident was sooner or later inevitable because of the extreme technical difficulty of drilling in water that is a mile deep. According to, Freudenberg and Gramling: "We appear to be at the very limits of our technological abilities, or even a little beyond."[15]

The Presidential Commission articulated a similar view:[16]

> "[Drilling 5,000 ft below the sea surface] is a complex and dazzling enterprise. The remarkable advances that have propelled the move to deepwater drilling merit comparison with exploring space. The Commission is respectful and admiring of the industry's technological capability.
>
> But drilling in deepwater brings new risk, not yet completely addressed by the reviews of where it is safe to drill, what could go wrong, and how to respond if something does go awry. The drilling rigs themselves bristle with potentially dangerous machinery. The deepwater environment is cold, dark, distant, and under high pressure … The *Deepwater Horizon* and Macondo well vividly illustrated all of those very real risks."

The Commission does not go so far as to say that the accident was inevitable but, in this passage, it appears to attribute the accident to the technical complexity of what was being attempted.

There is, however, one writer, Charles Perrow, who argues that deepwater drilling is so technically challenging that catastrophic accidents in this context are inevitable. Perrow first advanced this type of argument as a way of understanding the nuclear power plant accident at Three Mile Island in Pennsylvania in 1979. The technology, he said, was both complex and tightly coupled. Here is recent statement by Perrow of what this means:[17]

> "Interactive complexity is not simply many parts; it means that many of the parts can interact in ways no designer anticipated and no operator can understand. Since everything is subject to failure, the more complex the system the more opportunities for unexpected interactions of failures. Tight coupling means that failures can cascade through the system since the system cannot be stopped, fixed and restarted without damage; substitutions are not available, and failed subsystems cannot be isolated."

And, in the context of nuclear power plants, he writes:[18]

> "Because of the complexity of these plants and their tight coupling, serious accidents are inevitable, *even with the best management practices and attention to safety*."

The italicised words are in the original. No matter how well managed a plant may be, the technology makes accidents inevitable. For this reason, Perrow calls such accidents "normal accidents" in a book with this title. Three Mile Island was, he says, a normal accident in this sense.

The conclusion that Perrow draws from this is that, if the consequences of a normal accident are catastrophic, the technology should be abandoned. Perrow has long argued that nuclear power should be abandoned for this reason. Instead of nuclear power, we should look to more decentralised technologies, such as wind power and solar, where the consequences of failure are not disastrous.

The theory of normal accidents has proved very influential — undeservedly so, because there are insuperable problems with Perrow's analysis. First, it is almost impossible to identify other examples of normal accidents. All of the best known accidents of recent decades, for example, the space shuttle accidents, turn out to have been caused by poor management, rather than being the inevitable consequence of complexity and tight coupling. So the theory is of little use in explaining accidents that have actually occurred. Perrow himself recognises this.[19] But, even more damning for the theory, on re-examination, Three Mile Island turns out *not* to have been a normal accident.[20] There were prior warnings about everything that went wrong at Three Mile Island which management dismissed or paid no attention to. The Three Mile Island accident was really no different in this respect from all of the other major accidents that have been exhaustively studied; it does not require a special theory to explain it!

Be that as it may, Perrow has recently applied his analysis to deepwater drilling. He concludes:[21]

> "I … argue that deepwater drilling, especially in ecologically sensitive areas, should be abandoned, because it combines complexity and coupling with catastrophic potential."

Given this statement, one might have thought that Perrow would go on to treat Macondo as a normal accident. But *no*:[22]

> "I do not think that the failure on April 20, 2010 of the rig built by Transocean and run by BP was a system accident (or 'normal accident'). While such rigs are very complex and very tightly coupled, it is more likely that faulty executive decisions resulted in knowingly running unnecessary and dangerous risks."

So, again, normal accident theory proves to be irrelevant when it comes to explaining a particular accident of interest. Given the irrelevance of the theory of normal accidents to most, perhaps all, real accidents, the fact that the theory remains influential becomes itself a matter requiring explanation. To follow this up, however, would take us into the realm of the sociology of ideas, which is beyond the scope of this work.

Given the appeal of Perrow's work, it is not surprising that others have sought to apply it to the Macondo accident. According to Joel Achenbach, a journalist who followed the story closely as it unfolded:[23]

> "*Normal accidents* [the book and the theory] anticipates the *Deepwater Horizon* disaster to an eerie degree."

He goes on as follows:[24]

> "Perrow writes: 'In complex industrial, space, and military systems, the normal accident generally (not always) means that the interactions are not only unexpected, but are *incomprehensible* for some critical period of time'. This incomprehensibility goes with the territory in any technology, but it's exacerbated when crucial hardware is in a remote place — low earth orbit, say, or the deep sea. When the oil industry drills in shallow water, the blowout preventer is often right there on the deck of the rig or platform. When the industry goes into deep water, the blowout preventer migrates to the sea floor where it is out of reach. It may be visible in the camera of an ROV [remotely operated vehicle], but you can't walk up and poke it, can't fiddle with a three inch kill line to see if it's clogged. Depth matters. Viewed broadly, *the Deepwater Horizon accident should have been expected.*" (emphasis added)

Why? Because the technology was such that *this* accident was inevitable. This, in short, was a "normal accident".

What has happened here is that Achenbach has fallen into a trap that Perrow has inadvertently set for him. He has analysed the technology in Perrow's terms and, quite understandably, taken the additional step of treating this accident as a normal accident, something that Perrow himself refrained from doing.

But, quite apart from this, there is another significant problem with normal accident theory as Achenbach has tried to apply it. It is true that the Macondo accident is incomprehensible to the participants, once it is underway. Once oil, gas and mud began spewing onto the deck, there was bewilderment and chaos. Events at that point were tightly coupled and there were undoubtedly complex interactions occurring, especially with the blowout preventer. But the sequence of events *leading up* to the accident cannot be described in this way. The barrier failures were not tightly coupled. They involved human decisions at every step, and each of those decisions could have been different. There was plenty of time to prevent the blowout from occurring. Normal accident theory, then, adds nothing to our understanding of the causes of this accident, as Perrow himself recognises.

Chapter

11

To conclude this section, quite apart from the theory of normal accidents, the whole argument about technological complexity adds nothing to our understanding of the Macondo accident. As we have seen, the causes of the accident are rooted in fallible decision-making rather than fallible technology.

Conclusion

The popular writing about the Macondo incident does not provide us with much insight into its causes. On the whole, that was not its purpose. Much of it aims to put the incident into a broader environmental and political context. Some of it aims to provide an account of the blowout and its aftermath from the point of view of those who lived through it. But it is necessary to critically examine the casual explanations provided in these accounts because they represent widely held views which cannot be allowed to go unchallenged.

Endnotes

1   Reed and Fitzgerald, 2011, p xii.

2   Steffy, 2011, pp xvi, xvii, 240, 253.

3   Lehner and Deans, 2010, p 78.

4   Freudenburg and Gramling, 2011, p 42.

5   RiskMetrics Group, *Integrated oil and gas: operations, health and safety*, July 2010.

6   J Schmit, "BP could learn from Exxon's safety response to Valdez oil spill", *USA Today*, 3 August 2010.

7   Jonathan Tilove, *The Times-Picayune*, 13 October 2011.

8   See http://royaldutchshellplc.com. Shell also had a major oil leak in UK waters in August 2011. See *Shell's reputation hit by North Sea oil spill*, Associated Press, 16 August 2011.

9   ExxonMobil also suffered the hugely reputation-damaging *Exxon Valdez* disaster in 1989 and the widely publicised Longford gas plant accident in 1998.

10 OSC, p vii.

11 BBC interview, 9 November 2010.

12 Clarke, 1999.

13 OSC, p 84.

14 OSC, p 84.

15 Freudenberg and Gramling, p 164.

16 OSC, pp viii, ix.

17 This passage is an adaptation by Perrow from the preface to his most recent book (Perrow, 2011). It appeared in a blog at http://theenergycollective.com/davidlevy/40008/deepwater-oil-too-risky. Accessed 21 July 2011.

18 Perrow, 2011, p 172.

19 Perrow, 1994, p 218. Perrow restates his view in "Fukushima and the inevitability of accidents", published on 1 November 2011, at http://bos.sagepub.com/content/67/6/44. At one point in his

article, after discussing a number of well-known accidents, he says that "Three Mile Island is the only accident in my list that qualifies" as a normal accident.

20   Hopkins, 2001.

21   See the blog referenced above.

22   See the blog referenced above.

23   Achenbach, 2011, p 239.

24   Achenbach, 2011, pp 240, 241.

CHAPTER 12

CONCLUSION

The Macondo blowout took 11 lives and caused untold damage to the environment and to the livelihood of Gulf state residents. It was also enormously costly to BP, both in financial and reputational terms. This chapter is an overview of the human and organisational causes of the disaster. It provides the reader with a relatively self-contained summary of the arguments of the book.

Much of the popular writing about this tragedy treats BP as a reckless or rogue company, very different from all of the other major oil and gas companies. It is true that BP was more decentralised than the others, but the facts do not support an argument that it was especially reckless. Nor was the Macondo accident an inevitable consequence of operating at the limits of technology, as some writers have suggested. The causes of this accident were far more mundane, involving a series of human and organisational factors similar to those identified in other high-profile accidents. What makes this accident important, from an accident prevention point of view, is that the various inquiries laid bare the decision-making processes of the engineers and allowed us to examine the contribution of this group of professionals to the genesis of the accident. For this reason, the present analysis pays as much attention to these "back room" decisions as it does to the decisions of frontline personnel.

The failure of defence-in-depth

One of the striking things about the Macondo accident was the failure of the system of defence-in-depth. Defence-in-depth works on the assumption that the various defences are independent of each other. Thus, if there are two defences, each with a 10% probability of failure, the probability that both will fail together is only 1%. Adding further independent defences reduces the risk further. But, if the defences are not independent, if the failure of one somehow contributes to the failure of others, the system will not give the expected reduction in level of risk.

In fact, the system of defences at the Macondo well was highly interdependent. Some defences were undermined by the belief that earlier defences had worked, while some relied on the proper functioning of others and did not function effectively when the earlier defences failed. The image that comes most readily to mind is falling dominos. Once one fell, all of the others collapsed. Here is a summary of this interdependence (see Figure 12.1):

- Risks were taken with the first barrier, the cement job, on the assumption that the well integrity test would pick up any problems and that the blowout preventer (BOP) would operate as a last line of defence, if necessary.

- The cement evaluation tool was not used because the cement job was believed to have been successful. This barrier was always intended to be conditional in this way. Strictly speaking, it was not part of the system of *independent* barriers. Nevertheless, it fits the pattern of a barrier rendered ineffective by the belief that an earlier barrier had been successful.

- The well integrity test was undermined by the announcement that the cement job had been successful. This gave rise to a powerful confirmation bias on the part of the testers that led them to dismiss the indications of failure that they were getting.

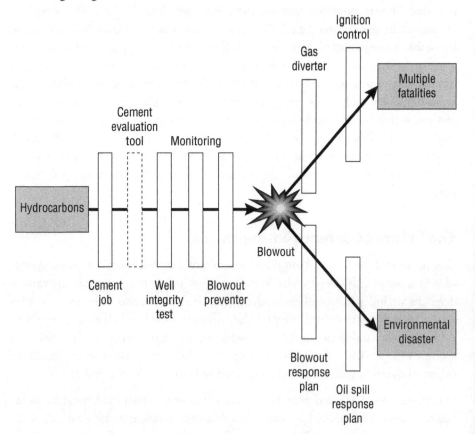

FIGURE 12.1: Barrier failures at the Macondo well

- The Macondo team effectively stopped monitoring the well in the last hours before the blowout because of the earlier declarations that the cement job had been successful and that the well had passed the integrity test.

- The BOP failed because it was designed on the assumption that operators would be monitoring the well vigilantly and would activate the device long before well fluids gushed out onto the rig. The monitoring failure therefore contributed directly to the failure of the BOP.

There were two sets of post-blowout consequences — the explosion and fatalities on the one hand, and the oil spill and environmental disaster on the other:

- With respect to the explosion, the diverter did not automatically divert overboard because no one had seriously imagined that all of the preceding defences would fail. BP and Transocean assumed that, if a catastrophic blowout were to occur, vigilant monitoring would provide an early warning and the crew would have been evacuated before the blowout erupted onto the deck of the rig. Accordingly, the procedures dealing with the use of the diverter were focused on avoiding small-scale spills of drilling fluid, rather than responding to a catastrophic blowout.

- The ignition prevention system failed because it was assumed that earlier defences would ensure that large quantities of gas would never be present in the engine room where they could ignite.

- With respect to the oil spill, there was no effective plan to cap the flowing well because it was assumed that a subsequent barrier, the oil spill response plan, would effectively contain the spill for many weeks while a relief well was drilled to intercept and block the flowing well.

- Finally, the oil spill response plan failed because BP was relying on pre-blowout barriers to avoid a catastrophic oil spill, and its oil spill response plan was written to satisfy regulatory requirements rather than with any real concern about how effective it might be.

Evidently, this was a failure of the system of defence-in-depth itself. There are some important lessons here. First, there is a general tendency for people to regard a single effective defence as good enough and to drop their guard if they believe that such a defence is in place. The reality is that no one defence can be relied on and all defences must be made to work as effectively as possible. A second lesson is that certain defences assume the successful operation of earlier defences. This was particularly the case with the BOP. This conditionality needs to be widely advertised. If everyone had realised that the effective operation of the BOP depended on vigilant monitoring, the Macondo crew may not have had such blind faith in the BOP.

Chapter

12

The failure of the system of defences is only part of the explanation for the Macondo tragedy. The following sections identify the human and organisational causes of several of these barrier failures.

The failure of the cement job

There were two aspects to the failure of the cement job. The first was that the engineers took various decisions that increased the risk of failure — indeed, in combination, caused the failure. The second was that they believed the cement job had been a success, and declared it to be so, based on a full returns test which provided information about only one of several possible failure modes. At least in retrospect, we can say that this was poor decision-making on the part of the engineers, as well as other members of the Macondo team. There are several factors that contributed to this poor engineering judgment. These factors are summarised in Figure 12.2. The reader is invited to relate the following text back to this diagram, using the numbers provided.

(1) The engineers recognised that their decisions increased the risk of cement failure. But they saw this as a commercial risk, not a safety risk. This was only plausible on the assumption that, if the cement job failed, they would know that it had failed and they would then take remedial action. In fact, they did not know that the cement job had failed and, in this way, the commercial risk became a safety risk. The failure to recognise that commercial risk could also create safety risk lies at the heart of their poor decision-making.

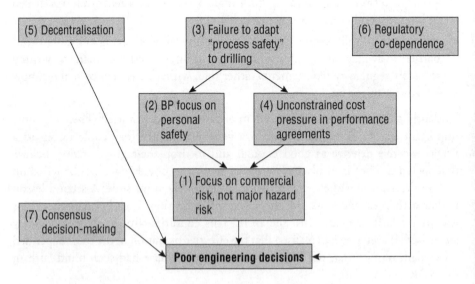

FIGURE 12.2: Factors leading to poor engineering decision-making

(2) One of the reasons for this failure to think carefully about safety risk was the very meaning that safety had for BP drilling operations. Since the Texas City disaster, we are accustomed to making the distinction between personal and process safety. The message from Texas City was that process and personal safety need to be measured and managed differently. But, in BP drilling operations, the whole concept of process safety and major hazard safety more generally tended to disappear from view, leaving only a focus on personal or occupational safety.

The management walk-around on the day of the Macondo accident illustrated this state of mind with devastating clarity. The executives involved in the walk-around were focused exclusively on personal safety; there was no discussion of major hazard risk. It is a truism that the culture of an organisation is determined by its leadership. From this point of view, it is entirely unsurprising that the engineers were as blind to major hazard risk as they were. Moreover, the activities of the Macondo engineers had no obvious implications for personal safety. As a result, neither personal nor process safety was relevant for them. Safety per se was simply not on their agenda as they went about designing the cement job.

(3) The blindness to major hazard risk is not unique to BP drilling operations, but there was a particular reason for it in this context. The concept of process safety was developed for process industries — refining and the like — where the issue is keeping dangerous substances contained in pipes and tanks, particularly substances that can cause major fires and explosions. On the other hand, in drilling operations, the most serious hazard is a blowout. The fact is that process safety, narrowly understood, is *not* directly applicable to drilling operations and needs to be adapted to deal with blowout risk. BP had not recognised the need to make this adaptation. So it was that major hazard risk tended to disappear from view, as far as the engineers were concerned.

(4) Cost pressure was another factor that contributed to the safety risk blindness of the Macondo engineers. There was enormous pressure on the Macondo team, both engineers and line managers, to keep costs to a minimum. The most obvious manifestation of this pressure was in their performance agreements. These agreements specified production and cost reduction goals, both for engineers and for line managers, and bonuses depended on how well these goals were met. This provided a strong incentive to take what were seen as commercial risks.

This cost pressure was not entirely unconstrained. Apart from production/cost reduction targets, performance agreements also included personal injury reduction targets. BP managers were very focused on personal safety, at least partly because of the injury reduction incentives contained in the company's remuneration system.

Chapter

12

But this did not extend to blowout risk. In the years immediately preceding the Macondo blowout, BP had been moving hesitantly towards including indicators of process safety in performance agreements. This culminated in 2010, when a numerical indicator of process safety was finally included in the performance agreements of top managers. That indicator was the number of losses of primary containment, defined in such a way as to emphasise gas leaks. But BP had made the mistake of seeking a single indicator of process safety across all of its operations and had not recognised that process safety indicators need to be relevant to the major hazards faced by particular operations or sites (see (3) in Figure 12.2). The rate of gas leaks or, more generally, losses of primary containment, does *not* measure how well a drilling operation is managing its risk of blowout. Accordingly, seeking to drive down this rate will not reduce the risk of blowout. In short, there was nothing in the performance agreements or the incentive system to focus attention on the risk of blowout. The result was that the pressure to cut costs was unconstrained by any countervailing pressure to attend to the most significant major hazard risk that they faced.

Let me put this as provocatively as possible by asking the following question: given that BP experienced a major accident event in the Gulf of Mexico, why did this happen in its drilling operations and not in its production operations? The answer that immediately suggests itself is that the indicator of major hazard risk that BP was using — losses of primary containment — was helping to drive down major hazard risk on production platforms, but could have no such effect on drilling platforms.

(5) BP's decentralised organisational design was a further factor that contributed to the lack of engineering rigour during the Macondo cement job. The Macondo engineering team reported to line management at a low level within the overall organisational structure. This meant that they were subordinated to these line managers and their cost concerns, and it meant that their performance agreements were designed by these relatively low-level and cost-focused line managers. This inevitably tended to corrupt good engineering judgment. BP had recognised this problem and was slowly reorganising itself so as to make engineers answerable to higher-level engineering managers in a process known as centralising the engineering function. But these changes were too late to make any difference to the Macondo engineers who were the last engineers in the Gulf of Mexico to be centralised in this way. Since the Macondo tragedy, BP has gone much further in imposing centralised control over its operations, suggesting that the company itself saw its decentralised organisational structure as one of the most significant causes of the Macondo blowout.

Again, let me ask a provocative question. The exploration drilling group was not the only BP drilling group in the Gulf of Mexico; there was also so-called development drilling going on. Why did a catastrophic blowout occur in the exploration drilling group, and not the others? One answer to this question is that this was the only group that had not been effectively centralised at the time of the accident.

(6) Regulatory co-dependence was a further contributing factor. The regulator tended to rely on BP engineers, assuming that they would have the necessary expertise to design and construct wells safely. On the other hand, BP engineers who wanted to modify a design in a way that they knew would increase the risk of failure relied on the regulator to authorise, or alternatively reject, whatever change they were proposing. Furthermore, they assumed that, if an authorisation was forthcoming, the proposed course of action must be acceptable. This was a process that meant that neither the regulator nor the operators accepted full responsibility for safe well design. So it was that the regulator rubber-stamped a number of last-minute changes that increased the risk of cement failure, without ensuring that there was any commensurate increase in attention to the detection of cement failures.[1]

(7) Consensus decision-making was also a problem. Decisions tended to be made by groups, and the test of whether the decision was a good one seemed to be whether everyone was "comfortable" with it. This meant that, in practice, no one person really took responsibility for decisions.

A comment on the diagram

Figure 12.2 is very different from barrier failure diagrams such as Figure 12.1. It focuses on just one of the barrier failures — the initial cement job failure and the associated declaration of success — and identifies a series of organisational factors that led to this failure. It can be seen as beginning to fill out the causal connections identified in Figure 1.3 — the extended Swiss cheese model. Readers will notice immediately that it inverts that model, putting the more remote organisational causes at the top of the figure, rather than the bottom. This is more a matter of convention than logic. The convention being followed here derives from "AcciMap" (accident map) analysis that depicts the more remote causes at higher levels. The AcciMap style of analysis was developed more fully in my book, *Lessons from Longford*.[2] However, Figure 12.1 does not display all of the features of an AcciMap. It is designed simply to summarise in an easy visual form the factors that led to poor engineering decision-making, and hence to the failure of the cement job and the associated erroneous declaration of success.

The failure of the well integrity test

The well integrity test involved reducing the pressure in the well to see if hydrocarbons would begin flowing upwards. They did, which meant that the well was not sealed and would blow out when the opportunity arose. However, the team doing the test misinterpreted the results and concluded that the well was secure. How could this have happened? Most analysts concluded that the problem was that BP had not developed sufficiently detailed procedures for carrying out the test. While this is true, it does not account for the fact that no one recognised the unambiguous evidence of failure that confronted them. As we saw in Chapter 3, a series of factors came into play. These are represented in Figure 12.3. As before, the numbers in the text refer to the numbers in the diagram.

(1) First and foremost, the group was subject to powerful confirmation bias because the cement job had already been declared a success. In these circumstances, they were not *testing* whether the well was safe, they were *confirming* that it was. This is a subtle but vital distinction. It meant that, when they got results suggesting otherwise, they repeated the test in various ways until finally they got a result that could be interpreted as a success, at which point, it was "mission accomplished".

(2) The power of this confirmation bias stemmed in part from the failure to understand or take seriously the principle of defence-in-depth. One successful barrier was enough for these men. The cement job had already been declared a success and, in their minds, the well integrity test was almost redundant.

(3) Furthermore, the team had a very limited idea of what they were doing — their mental model was deficient. They conducted tests on two different flow lines

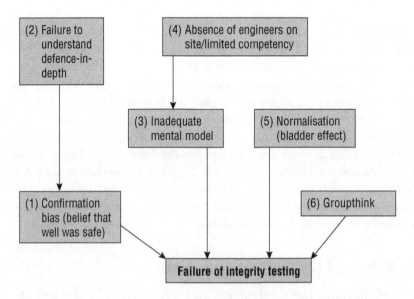

FIGURE 12.3: Factors leading to the failure of the well integrity test

running into the same cavity beneath the BOP. The results should have been identical, but they weren't. The team failed to understand that this was a serious anomaly.

(4) The group's limited mental model of what was going on was a result of their limited professional competence, and of the fact that there were no professional engineers on site who were able to provide advice on what was happening.

(5) Next, the team was able to rationalise the different outcomes on the two flow lines as being a result of a so-called "bladder effect". Experts deny that such an effect exists but, in the minds of those present, the bladder effect helped them *normalise* the discrepancy between the results on the two lines.

(6) Finally, those in the group who remained doubtful of the interpretation that was being placed on the results were silenced by a powerful groupthink process in which the informal group leaders, who happened to be Transocean drillers, prevailed over the formal decision-makers, the BP staff men.

So it was that the team came to the conclusion that the well had passed the integrity test, when in fact it had failed.

Failure to monitor

In preparation for departure, the crew of the *Deepwater Horizon* had to replace all of the drilling fluid in the riser with seawater. The riser, it will be remembered, is the section of piping between the sea floor and the rig. After this replacement operation, the crew would then remove the riser itself. While replacement is occurring, the flow of seawater into the riser should exactly match the outflow of drilling fluid. If more is coming out than is going in, hydrocarbons must be flowing in at the bottom of the well. To ensure that this is not happening, the crew was supposed to monitor inflows and outflows continuously. But they failed to do so. During much of this period, they were not directing the outflowing mud into a tank where it could be measured. Instead, they were diverting it directly overboard into the tanks of a supply vessel. This meant that it was practically impossible for the specialist mud monitoring personnel to do their job. In the last stages of the operation, for reasons that are not relevant here, the crew was diverting the outflow from the well into the sea. It was during this period that the outflow from the well began to exceed inflow but, because there was no effective monitoring occurring, no one recognised what was happening until mud began spewing out of the well onto the rig. This failure to monitor was due to several factors, summarised in Figure 12.4.

(1) The crew was engaged in simultaneous operations in order to get the job finished as quickly as possible. For instance, they were off-loading the mud directly to the supply vessel so that they could get on with cleaning operations aboard the *Deepwater Horizon*.

Chapter

12

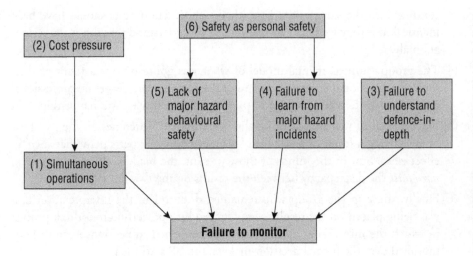

FIGURE 12.4: Factors leading to failure to monitor

(2) Their sense of urgency was exacerbated by the fact that the job was way past its scheduled completion date, which generated powerful cost pressures.

(3) There was no commitment to the philosophy of defence-in-depth. The well had twice been declared safe which, in the minds of many of those present, meant that careful monitoring was now superfluous and could be abandoned in the interest of speeding up the process.

(4) There was a striking failure to learn from a very similar incident that had happened to a Transocean drilling rig four months earlier in United Kingdom waters. The lesson from that event was that there is a need for vigilant monitoring to the very end of the operation. There had been no attempt, however, to communicate this lesson to the Gulf of Mexico.

(5) BP and Transocean assumed that line managers would ensure that staff followed well control procedures and there were no independent systems for checking on whether this was the case. There were various safe behaviour programs designed to reinforce *personal* safety, but no equivalent programs to ensure safe behaviour with respect to major hazards.

The two preceding paragraphs identified two contributory factors: the absence of any attempt to learn process lessons from another relevant incident; and the lack of behavioural safety programs in relation to process safety. Both of these failures stem from the way that safety was conceptualised as personal safety, ignoring process safety or major hazard risk (see (6) in Figure 12.4). This risk-blindness was shared by both BP and Transocean.

Finally, let us again ask a question that highlights a central issue: why did the Macondo blowout occur at this late stage of the operation, after drilling had been completed and a cement job had been carried out, apparently successfully? The answer would seem to be that this is the time at which everyone tends to drop their guard. This is therefore the most dangerous time in the whole operation.

Failure of risk assessment

The remaining barrier failures have not been traced back to their organisational causes in quite the same way as earlier barriers. One thing stands out about them, however: they all involve a failure of the risk management process.

This is the best way to think about the failure of the BOP. The effective functioning of the BOP depended on vigilant monitoring and early operator intervention. This was a significant design limitation. One can infer from the behaviour of the crew that they had no idea how critical their behaviour was to the effective operation of the BOP. The lesson here is that protective equipment should function as automatically as possible, rather than depending on operators to take the appropriate actions. If this is not possible, then people need to be trained to understand the design assumptions that are built into the equipment they use, and to recognise that human error can completely undermine the value of protective equipment.

The post-blowout barrier failures show a similar failure of the risk management process when it comes to rare but catastrophic events. The safety risk assessments did not take account of the possibility of multiple fatalities because they assumed that people would have been evacuated before a major blowout occurred. Moreover, BP's failure to take seriously the possibility of a blowout causing multiple fatalities was justified on the basis that such an event had never occurred before in the industry. This is unsatisfactory. Designers of major hazard facilities must consider all conceivable catastrophic events, not just catastrophic events that have previously occurred. That is the lesson of the Macondo blowout and of the Fukushima nuclear disaster. Furthermore, if risk analysts end up taking the view that a particular catastrophic event is so unlikely that it is not cost-effective to protect against it, this decision should be made public, so that others can scrutinise and, if necessary, challenge it. The sad fact about the Macondo risk assessments is that they were never subject to this wider scrutiny and challenge.

As for the environmental aspects of the risk assessment, BP could not say that an environmentally catastrophic oil spill was unknown in the industry. But its environmental risk assessment was just as inadequate as its safety risk assessment. It assumed that, in the event of a blowout, the oil spill response plan would effectively contain the oil until a relief well could be drilled to intersect and block the blowout well. There was therefore no need to think about how the well might be capped more quickly. As it turned out, the oil spill response plan was woefully inadequate and was no more than a paper exercise designed to fulfill a regulatory requirement. It is evident that BP had not carefully considered the possibility of this kind of rare but catastrophic event and had no effective strategy for dealing with it.

BP and Transocean were very focused on low-consequence high-frequency events, from both a safety point of view (slips, trips and falls) and an environmental point of view (small spills). But there was much less focus on high-consequence low-frequency events. The tendency here was to do whatever was necessary to satisfy regulatory requirements, but no more. BP supplied the necessary paperwork to the regulator but, unfortunately, the regulator was not resourced to scrutinise these documents closely or to challenge the assumptions that they contained. The assumptions and biases contained within these risk assessments therefore lay undisturbed, until the Macondo incident caused the spotlight to be shone on them.

The regulator is really the first line of public scrutiny. Usually, it is also the last. It is therefore important that regulators do their utmost to check the reasoning that underlies the risk assessments of rare but catastrophic events.

Consensus decision-making

One social process that contributed both to poor engineering decision-making and to the failure of the well integrity test was consensus decision-making. For the engineers, the test of whether a decision was the right one seemed to be whether everyone was "comfortable" with it. This meant that no one person took real responsibility for decisions. Even the management of change process, which involved numerous signatures, appeared to diffuse responsibility to the point that no one accepted real responsibility for the final decision. In the case of the well integrity test, a powerful groupthink process was at work that completely overwhelmed the company man who was formally responsible for the decision.

Many companies aspire to single-point accountability for decisions, on the assumption that it makes for more conscientious decision-making. This needs to be made a social reality, not just a legal formula. If the decision-maker is to be as effective as possible, this person must be isolated to some extent from group processes. This does not mean that decision-makers should act in isolation. They of course need to consult, but consultation must be kept conceptually distinct from decision-making. In principle, the decision-maker must in some sense withdraw before making the decision.

Storytelling

Many accidents are disturbingly similar to previous occurrences, which means that the lessons of those previous events have not been assimilated. It is not enough to send out bulletins about lessons learnt. Companies must ensure that their staff have really learnt the relevant lessons. One way to do this is to tell and retell the stories of previous events so that people are sensitised to the mistakes of the past and can recognise the precursor events when they occur. Because catastrophic events are beyond the direct experience of most people, learning from one's own experience is generally not an option; one must learn from the experience of others. Storytelling was one of the most important means of instruction in pre-literate societies. In an era where information is transmitted at ever-increasing rates, taking time to tell the stories is still a vital means of ensuring that lessons are learnt.

Regulation

The regulator in the Gulf of Mexico had, to a large extent, been captured by the companies that it was supposed to regulate. This was a direct outcome of political and funding decisions in Washington. As a result, it tended to acquiesce in whatever companies wanted. Moreover, its program of inspections was somewhat ritualistic in character, and certainly not focused on how well companies were managing risk. Chapter 10 argued for the establishment of a safety case regime on the understanding that such a regime has four features: it employs a risk management framework; it requires the operator to make the case for safety to the regulator; it is implemented by a competent and independent regulator; and it is backed by a legal requirement that operators reduce risk so far as is reasonably practicable. Such regimes can be further improved by focusing on the organisational causes of accidents, such as those identified in this book.

Lessons

The preceding findings can be summarised from another point of view, namely, by identifying lessons that can be drawn from the Macondo event.

For companies:

- Where there is the potential for catastrophe, companies should focus on major hazard risk quite independently of personal safety risk.
- Commercial risk can create safety risk.
- Staff must understand and act in accordance with the philosophy of defence-in-depth.
- There should be centralised functional lines of authority that run to the top of the corporation.
- Indicators of major hazard risk cannot be generic and need to be specific to particular hazards.

- Remuneration systems should include relevant indicators of major hazard risk.
- Single-point accountability for decisions needs to be a social reality, not just a legal formula. This means, among other things, that decision-making must be distinguished from consultation.
- Behavioural safety programs should be extended to cover major hazard risk.
- Anomalies that resolve themselves with no immediate negative consequences should not be dismissed; they should be treated as warnings.
- The number of authorised deviations from standards, and the number of safety bypasses in place, should be treated as performance indicators to be driven downwards.
- Executive managers need to go into the field and ask the right questions to find out whether their policies are working in practice. These questions may be designed to elicit views from lower-level employees and/or they may be targeted in such a way as to audit major hazard risk controls.
- Companies need to develop better learning strategies.
- Risk assessments for low-probability catastrophic scenarios often contain critical assumptions that need to be highlighted and perhaps challenged.
- These lessons need to be understood by people at the very top of corporations, since it is they who have the power to implement them.

For governments:

- Governments should establish well-resourced safety case regimes.

For regulators:

- Regulators need to carefully scrutinise and challenge company risk assessments.
- Regulators should challenge companies to demonstrate that their remuneration systems effectively direct attention to major hazard risk. In particular, they should require companies to demonstrate that the performance agreements of top executives are appropriately focused on major hazard risk. (There is a good argument that the performance agreements of senior executives should be made public, subject to editing to remove truly confidential information.)
- Regulators should challenge companies to demonstrate that their organisational structures are appropriate for managing major hazards.

This is not intended as an exhaustive list of requirements for the management of major hazards. It is simply a selection of lessons that emerge with particular clarity from the Macondo disaster.

Endnotes

1 See BOEMRE, Appendix I.
2 Hopkins, 2000; see also Rasmussen, 1997, and Branford et al, 2009.

Chapter

12

APPENDIX 1

The decision tree

(Source: Appendix L of the BOEMRE report)

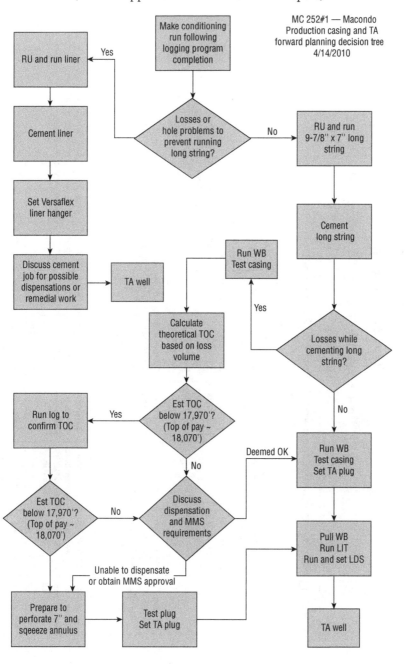

MC 252#1 — Macondo
Production casing and TA
forward planning decision tree
4/14/2010

APPENDIX 2

The BP risk matrix

(Source: Appendix J of the BOEMRE report)

Risk Rating Matrix — customise the matrix in the SETUP worksheet

Impact Level	Type of Impact										
	Health & Safety	Environment: Threats	Environment: Opportunities	Reputation: Threats	Reputation: Opportunities	Cost	Schedule	Production	Reserves	NPV	
	One or more fatalities	Damage long-term and/or extensive	—	Outrage. Prosecution. Possible loss of operating license	Commended by NGO at international level. Global recognition	> 10 $M	> 12.75 days	> 0.1 of Project Production*	> 0.15 of Project Reserves*	> 0.1 of Project NPV*	Very High
	Serious injury or DAFWC. HiPo	Short-term damage within facility boundary	Long-term and/or extensive improvement	Involvement of regulator	Commended by NGO at national level. Recognition within country	3-10 $M	3.4-12.75 days	0.03-0.1 of Project Production*	0.04-0.15 of Project Reserves*	0.03-0.1 of Project NPV*	High
	Recordable injury, first aid, serious occurrence	Rapid on-site clean-up	Short-term improvement within facility boundary	Complaints from local community	Commended by NGO at local level. Recognition within area	1-3 $M	0.85-3.4 days	0.01-0.03 of Project Production*	0.01-0.04 of Project Reserves*	0.01-0.03 of Project NPV*	Medium
	No impact	No impact	Minor enhancement	Minimal impact	Recognised positive contribution within BP	< 1 $M	< 0.85 days	< 0.01 of Project Production*	< 0.01 of Project Reserves*	< 0.01 of Project NPV*	Low

Probability/Frequency

Prob-Impact Grid

Impact Level	Very Low < 1%	Low 1–5%	Moderate 5–25%	High > 25%
Very High	Mod.	High	V. High	V. High
High	Low	Mod.	High	V. High
Medium	V. Low	Low	Mod.	High
Low	V. Low	V. Low	Low	Mod.

Probability

Very Low	Could only occur as the result of multiple, independent system or control failures. Future occurrence is thought most unlikely. No comparable occurrence is known.
Low	Could result from a plausible combination of system or control failures. Would probably occur if the system were to be operated for long enough. Comparable events are known to have occurred in the past.
Moderate	Could result from the failure of a single system or control. Could be expected to occur if this operation were repeated regularly. Comparable events are within the team's direct experience.
High	Uncontrolled. Will occur whenever circumstances are unfavourable. Comparable events are frequent.

Manageability

Low	Project Management Team can only influence impact. Risk reduction measures are unlikely to be cost-effective.
Medium	Project Management Team can influence probability and/or impact. Risk reduction measures will be roughly cost-neutral.
High	Project Management Team can control probability and/or impact. Risk reduction measures will be highly cost-effective.

BIBLIOGRAPHY

Achenbach, J, *A hole at the bottom of the sea: the race to kill the BP oil gusher*, Simon and Schuster, New York, 2011.

Argoteand, L & Todrova, G, "Organisational learning", *International Review of Industrial and Organisational Psychology*, Wiley, New York, 2007, vol 22, ch 5, pp 193–234.

Baker, J et al, *The report of the BP US refineries independent safety review panel*, BP, London, 2007.

Bergin, T, *Spills and spin: the inside story of BP*, Random House, London, 2011.

Bice, M & Hayes, J, Risk management: from hazard logs to bow ties", in A Hopkins (ed), *Learning from high reliability organisations*, CCH Australia Limited, Sydney, 2009.

BOEMRE [Bureau of Ocean Energy Management, Regulation and Enforcement], *Report regarding the causes of the April 20, 2010 Macondo well blowout*, US Department of the Interior, Washington, 2011.

BP, *Deepwater Horizon accident investigation report*, September 2010.

BP, Submission to the National Academy of Engineers, 2011 (NAE Public Access File, #188-2).

Branford, K, Naikar, N & Hopkins, A, "Guidelines for AcciMap analysis", in A Hopkins (ed), *Learning from high reliability organisations*, CCH Australia Limited, Sydney, 2009.

Buckner, T, "Is management by wandering around still relevant?", *Exchange Magazine*, May/June 2008, pp 86–88.

Burk, M et al, "The dread factor: how hazards and safety training influence learning and performance", *Journal of Applied Psychology* 2011, 96(1): 46–70.

CAIB [Columbia Accident Investigation Board], Report, vol 1, National Aeronautics and Space Administration, Washington, 2003.

CCR [Chief Counsel for the National Commission on the BP Deepwater Horizon Oil Spill and Offshore Drilling], Report, CCR, Washington, 2011.

Clarke, L, *Mission improbable*, University of Chicago Press, Chicago, 1999.

CSB [US Chemical Safety Board], *Investigation report: refinery explosion and fire*, CSB, Washington, 2007.

Diener, D, *Introduction to well control*, University of Texas, Austin, 1999.

DWI [Deepwater Investigation], transcript from the joint BOEMRE/Coast Guard inquiry, originally available at www.deepwaterinvestigation.com.

Flin, R, O'Connor, P & Crichton, M, *Safety at the sharp end: a guide to non-technical skills*, Ashgate Publishing, Surrey, 2008.

Frankel, A, *Patient safety rounds: a how-to workbook*, Joint Commission on Accreditation of Healthcare Organizations, 2008.

Freudenburg, W & Gramling, R, *Blowout in the Gulf*, MIT Press, Cambridge, Massachusetts, 2011.

Garfinkle, H, *Studies in ethnomethodology*, Prentice Hall, Englewood Cliffs, New Jersey, 1967.

Haddon-Cave, C, *The Nimrod review*, Her Majesty's Stationery Office, London, 28 October 2009.

Hayes, J, Operational decision-making, in A Hopkins (ed), *Learning from high reliability organisations*, CCH Australia Limited, Sydney, 2009.

Hayes, J, "Use of safety barriers in operational safety decision making", *Safety Science* 2012, 50(3): 424–432.

Hayes, J, "Operator competence and capacity — lessons from the Montara blowout", *Safety Science* 2012a, 50: 563–574.

Hays, S, "Structure and agency and the sticky problem of culture", *Sociological Theory* 1994, 12(1): 57–72.

Hilmer, F & Donaldson, L, *Management redeemed: debunking the fads that undermine corporate performance*, Free Press, East Roseville, NSW, 1996.

Hopkins, A, *Lessons from Longford: the Esso gas plant explosion*, CCH Australia Limited, Sydney, 2000.

Hopkins, A, "A culture of denial: sociological similarities between the Moura and Gretley mine disasters", *Journal of Occupational Health and Safety — Australia and New Zealand* 2000a, 16(1): 29–36.

Hopkins, A, "Was Three Mile Island a normal accident?", *Journal of Contingencies and Crisis Management* 2001, 9(2): 65–72.

Hopkins, A, "Two models of major hazard regulation: recent Australian experience", in B Kirwan, A Hale & A Hopkins (eds), *Changing regulation: controlling risks in society*, Pergamon, Amsterdam, 2002.

Hopkins, A, "What are we to make of safe behaviour programs?", *Safety Science* 2006, 44: 583–597.

Hopkins, A, "Beyond compliance monitoring: new strategies for safety regulators", *Law and Policy* 2007, 29(2): 210–225.

Hopkins, A, *Failure to learn: the BP Texas City Refinery disaster*, CCH Australia Limited, Sydney, 2008.

Hopkins, A (ed), *Learning from high reliability organisations*, CCH Australia Limited, Sydney, 2009.

Hopkins, A, "Thinking about process safety indicators", *Safety Science* 2009a, 47: 460–465.

Hopkins, A, "Risk-management and rule-compliance: decision-making in hazardous industries", *Safety Science* 2011, 49: 110–120.

Hopkins, A, "Management walk-arounds: lessons from the Gulf of Mexico oil well blowout", *Safety Science* 2011a, 49: 1421–1425.

Hudson, P, van der Graaf, G & Bryden, R, *The rule of three: situational awareness in hazardous situations*, Society of Petroleum Engineers, SPE 46765.

Izon, D, Danenberger, E & Mayes, M, "Absence of fatalities in blowouts encouraging in MMS study of OCS incidents 1992–2006", *Drilling Contractor*, July/August 2007, pp 84–90.

Janis, I, *Groupthink: psychological studies of policy decisions and fiascos*, Houghton Mifflin, Boston, 1982.

King, J, "Letter to the editor regarding management walk-arounds: lessons from the Gulf of Mexico oil well blowout", *Safety Science* 2012, 50(3): 535.

Klein, G, *Streetlights and shadows*, MIT Press, Cambridge, Massachusetts, 2009.

Kletz, T, *Learning from accidents*, Gulf Professional Publishing, Oxford, 2001.

Lawson, M, "In praise of slack: time is of the essence", *The Academy of Management Executive* 2001, 15(3): 125.

Lefrancois, GR, *Psychology for teaching*, Wadsworth, Belmont, California,1994.

Lehner, P & Deans, B, *In deep water*, The Experiment, New York, 2010.

Leveson, N, "The use of safety cases in certification and regulation", *MIT ESD technical report*, 2011, website at http://sunnyday.mit.edu/safer-world.

Moghadden, M, *Social psychology*, Freeman, New York, 1998.

Nickerson, R, "Confirmation bias: a ubiquitous phenomenon in many guises", *Review of General Psychology* 1998, 2(2): 175–220.

OSC [National Commission on the BP Deepwater Horizon Oil Spill and Offshore Drilling], *Deepwater: the Gulf oil disaster and the future of offshore drilling, Report to the President*, January 2011.

Perrow, C, "The limits of safety: the enhancement of a theory of accidents", *Journal of Contingencies and Crisis Management* 1994, 4(2): 212–220.

Perrow, C, *Normal accidents*, Princeton University Press, Princeton, New Jersey, 1999.

Perrow, C, *The next catastrophe: reducing our vulnerabilities to natural, industrial and terrorist disasters*, Princeton University Press, Princeton, New Jersey, 2011.

Peters, T & Waterman, R, *In search of excellence: lessons from America's best run companies*, Harper and Row, New York, 1982.

Pickering, A & Cowley, S, "Risk matrices: implied accuracy and false assumptions", *Journal of Health & Safety Research and Practice* 2011, 2(1): 9–16.

Rasmussen, J, "Risk management in a dynamic society: a modelling problem", *Safety Science* 1997, 27(2-3): 183–213.

Reason, J, *Human error*, Cambridge University Press, Cambridge, 1990.

Reason J, *Managing the risks of organisational accidents*, Ashgate, Aldershot, 1997.

Reason, J, "Human error: models and management", *British Medical Journal* 2000, 320: 768–770.

Reed, S & Fitzgerald, A, *In too deep*, Bloomberg, Hoboken, 2011.

Salmon, PM, Stanton, NA & Young, KL, "Situation awareness on the road: review, theoretical and methodological issues, and future directions", *Theoretical Issues in Ergonomics Science*, 24 May 2011, pp 1–21.

Skogdalen, J, Utne, I & Vinnem, J, "Developing safety indicators for preventing offshore oil and gas deepwater drilling blowouts", *Safety Science* 2011, 49(8-9): 1187–1199.

Snook, S, *Friendly fire: the accidental shootdown of US Black Hawks over Northern Iraq*, Princeton University Press, Princeton, New Jersey, 2000.

Steffy, L, *Drowning in oil: BP and the reckless pursuit of profit*, McGraw Hill, New York, 2011.

Transocean, *Macondo well incident: Transocean investigation report*, vol 1, June 2011.

Vaughan, D, *The Challenger launch decision: risky technology, culture and deviance at NASA*, University of Chicago Press, Chicago, 1996.

Weick, K & Sutcliffe, K, *Managing the unexpected*, Jossey Bass, San Francisco, 2001.

Weick, K & Sutcliffe, K, *Managing the unexpected: resilient performance in an age of uncertainty*, Jossey Bass, San Francisco, 2007.

Yetton, P & Bottger, P, "Individual versus group problem solving: an empirical test of a best-member strategy", *Organisational Behaviour and Human Performance* 1982, 29(3): 307–321.

INDEX